Lee Jackson's
Carp Clinic

The ultimate guide to catching carp

Edited by Martin Ford

emap.

Produced by
Publishing Promotions
1 High Street
Princes Risborough
Bucks HP27 0AG

Published by
Emap Pursuit Publishing Ltd
Bretton Court
Bretton
Peterborough PE3 8DZ

Written by Lee Jackson and
Martin Ford 2001.

The author would like to thank
the following for their
assistance with this book:

Kevin and Gary Peet,
The Tackle Box,
Dartford,
Kent

Danny Fairbrass,
Korda Tackle

Jan Porter,
Shimano UK Ltd

Paul Reeves,
Fox International

Martin Locke,
Solar Tackle

Bob Baker,
Richworth

Peter Drennan,
Drennan International

Adam Penning,
E.S.P.

Pictures by Fiona Spencer,
Emap Studio, Martin Ford
and Lee Jackson.

Welcome to the world of carp fishing

This is my first in-depth book on carp angling … and it's packed with practical information that will take your carp fishing forward.

You can be as enthusiastic as you like, but if you're not utilising the right equipment, presentation and bait, in the correct way, your chances of catching carp will be greatly reduced.

Look and learn through these pages. Take these new found skills to the waterside and put them into practice, in your pursuit of carp.

Lee Jackson

This book is for my wife Helen and my three children Zoe, Kelly and Barry.
I thank them for their understanding of my time-consuming hobby. Thanks to Gary and Kevin Peet, co-owners of the Tackle Box, Dartford, Kent for giving me the opportunity of making a living from my hobby. Thanks also to Martin Ford of *Improve your Course Fishing* for help with this book and his friendship.

Contents

Catch those carp ...

The story of carp fishing

Carp are not new to this country – they were first used as a food supply for monks in ancient times

As far as I am aware, the first stockings of carp into this country were back in ancient times by monks who brought them in from the Continent and stocked them into their monastery stew ponds for the table.

These were the early carp fishers and, no doubt, they would have fished for them using very crude tackle, such as bamboo canes for fishing rods, although most of the time they would have been fishing for their supper rather than for the sport of it. I suspect though that even at this early stage in the history of carp fishing, they cannot have failed to recognise the hard fighting qualities of the carp they caught.

Some early references to bigger carp indicate that carp angling was active as early as 1739, when a carp of 13lb was reported from the River Thames, near Hampton Court. But the true spirit of carp angling really came to life in 1907, when an angler called H. S. Locksmith landed a carp of 19.5lb from the Weybridge canal. This fish was accepted as the biggest rod and line carp caught in Britain and was taken on honey paste.

Through the years to follow, a number of anglers would be single-handedly pioneering the art of fishing for and catching carp. Anglers like Albert Buckley who, at one time, held the British record with a carp of 26lb which he caught from Mapperley Reservoir, Derbyshire, in the 1930s.

During these early years, carp fishing must have been really difficult, not only because of the lack of suitable tackle but also because of the lack of waters that actually contained the fish.

I can hardly imagine the excitement that these anglers must have felt at hooking and actually landing a carp. Or perhaps I can, and that's why I have been a carp fisher for over 30 years and am constantly in pursuit of that next bite and that much hoped-for whacker.

Into the 1950s and the real carp fishing pioneers were born. Anglers began teaming up and pitting their wits against the wily carp, figuring that two or three brains would

◄ *Just a few of the many books on carp fishing that are a good point of reference.*

▲ *Lee returns a specimen carp caught by design.*

offer a lot more chance than just one.

Amongst others, the dynamic trio of Walker, Thomas and Richards were paving the way for carp fishing of the future. At this time many innovations were made that would go a long way towards making things easier for carp fishers.

What was really being driven home by anglers like these was that it was possible to go out and intentionally fish for, and catch carp, which was something that most anglers had thought impossible.

The reckoning was that the tackle needed in order to be able to land one of these great fish would have to be so strong that a clever old fish such as a carp would never fall for it in the first place. Walker and Co. proved the doubters wrong, and their catches were legendary. These culminated firstly in a new British record of 31lb to one of the team and then, in September 1952, in a 44lb common carp falling to the rod of the great Dick Walker, a fish that was to hold record status for many years.

This fish, which was known as 'Clarissa', ('Ravioli' to Walker) was to spend the rest of its life in the aquarium at London Zoo in Regent's Park. I can remember as a youngster staring in total amazement at this colossal fish. I imagined carp of these proportions swimming around beneath the watery depths of my local Dartford lakes, but doubted if such a monster could ever be hooked and played, let alone landed.

Clarissa the monster carp

Who would have believed that a small water like Redmire would produce not one, but two record fish of such large proportions? When Walker caught Clarissa at 44lb in 1952, it was thought that it wasn't possible for carp to attain such a weight. In the years that followed, another monster carp was getting ready to put in an appearance at an even bigger weight.

During its heyday, Redmire was visited by most well-known carp anglers. Many failed to catch, but all were caught by the magic of this mysterious little water. The small pool that housed those great record captures is still there today and is controlled by the Carp Society for its members.

Never in a million years would I have believed that in years to come I would actually land a few carp that would top this enormous fish.

This is not meant as a boast, but more to emphasise that with total determination, commitment and motivation, anyone reading *Carp Clinic* could aspire to the same.

I am lucky enough to have fished Redmire in recent years, as it's now under the management of the Carp Society, and although the monsters are no longer in existence, the magic certainly remains.

Surrounded by swims that are named after some of the legends that have fished it, such as Kefford's, Ingham's, Cranstoun's and Climo's to name just a few, to me it made Jackson's Swim at Darenth Tip Lake pale into insignificance. Although perhaps there is some young upstart out there who feels a certain amount of magic when fishing on my swim whilst playing with his Game Boy and waiting for a bite!

Redmire! It's amazing that a tiny pool deep in the Herefordshire hills could make such an enormous impact on the world of carp fishing.

Into the 1960s, at the time the Beatles were making their mark in music, water authorities were starting to stock waters with carp and, in particular in my area, the Kent River Board was really going to town.

As I sat waiting for my old porcupine quill float to dip and another roach, perch or whatever to make its way to the bank, I started to notice strange, mysterious-looking characters, who began to appear on the bank side. Dressed in camouflage clothing and looking as if they were going to war, these people had a strange way about them, to such an extent that you were frightened to talk to them. If you did, you were often totally ignored.

These were the next generation of carpers. In amongst their ranks were probably some very famous names, the likes of Jack Hilton, Tom Mintram, Bill Quinlan, Len Arbury and Jim Gibbinson.

In a relatively short period, carp fishing had come a long way. Anglers were abandoning their split-cane rods in favour of hollow fibreglass.

Mitchell reels were being used and the carp world's first proper bite alarm was born – the Heron Bite Indicator, which was actually an improved version of the alarm Richard Walker had helped design with Jack Opie a few years earlier.

Carp anglers of this period were very quiet about how they went about their business, and because they were going through a very big learning curve with a lot of experimentation taking place, they were extremely secretive about their findings if they were onto something that they felt would offer them an advantage.

Bait was an area that was receiving a great deal of thought. Whereas previously most carp fishing had taken place using various forms of bread or partly boiled potatoes, carp anglers were now experimenting with a variety of different baits in a very big way.

In particular, in my area of Kent, there was a lot of success being had on baits which were to become known as 'Specials'. In the late 1960s, when the cat finally got out of the bag, specials were starting to be written

▲ *Early books on carp fishing were a source of information for the keen beginner to the sport.*

about in the angling press by carp anglers such as Jim Gibbinson and Gerry Savage.

Predominantly, these baits were based on various cat and dog foods as well as things like sausage meat and beefburgers. A big favourite was a large tin of Kit-E-Kat catfood mixed with Pomenteg groundbait to make it into a paste.

At about the same time as this, the divorce rate amongst the carp fraternity started to increase. Was this due to the increasing amount of time that these anglers were spending away from home in pursuit of their quarry, or was it the smell that was starting to linger in the kitchen?

More and more carp waters were starting to spring up. This was especially noticeable in the south of the country due to the stocking policies of the water authorities.

More famous names were starting to appear in print – Billing Aquadrome, Ashlea Pool, the Dagenham pits, Horton Kirby, Brooklands Lakes, Cheshunt and that famous stretch of the River Nene known as the Electricity Cut, in Peterborough.

Redmire Pool, however, still remained at the top of the tree, and many innovations were still being made there.

One very young angler by the name of Rod Hutchinson was certainly starting to make his mark on the carp world.

He'd tried all the specials as well as bread, maggots and various other baits and, although having some success, this was nothing compared with the impact that he was to make with tiny seed baits such as hemp, tares, daris and various beans and peas such as maples, black eyed beans and chickpeas.

Particle bait fishing was born, and in the years to follow – and right up to this very

day – some phenomenal catches have been made using this approach.

Carp were now even being caught during the winter, something most anglers had reckoned impossible, as it was thought that carp buried themselves in the mud and hibernated until springtime. Things really were moving forward at an extremely fast pace.

Early in the 1970s another major breakthrough came about – boilies.

Now I'm not exactly sure who was the originator of these, but I would make an educated guess and say that it probably stemmed from the extensive bait experimentations of that quiet Kentishman, Fred Wilton.

Fred's theories were that if you could formulate a bait that offered the carp all of its nutritional requirements in a tiny package then, with careful prebaiting, it would be possible to wean

Pioneer of carp fishing

One man was to stand out of the crowd as a true pioneer of carp fishing. His name was Richard Stuart Walker and he was born in 1918 at 16 Fishponds Road, Hitchin, Hertfordshire. He was to play a major role in carp fishing up to and after the capture of his record carp which weighed 44lb and was caught on 12 September 1952 from Redmire Pool. Walker paved the way for the carp anglers of today with his ideas and often outspoken views. As an author and angler, he is remembered by all those that met or corresponded with him.

When he died following a long illness in 1985, the carp world lost a great man who had inspired so many to follow in his footsteps and enter the world of carp fishing.

▲ *Boilies and special hook patterns play a major role in modern-day carp angling.*

the carp off of all other foods and onto this bait as a preference.

Certainly, from the catches that Fred had made on various waters that he fished, this theory was proving very sound.

One thing that was felt very important with this type of bait was that it should, as much as possible, be able to resist the attentions of smaller species such as bream, roach and tench. So for this reason, the balls of bait were dropped into boiling water and boiled for a minute or so in order to form a tough skin on the outside.

All of these baits were made from high protein powders, and instead of water, eggs were used in order that the bait would bind together better, and so that a tougher skin would be formed when boiled. Well done, that man Fred Wilton. Although I never met you, I sincerely wish I had.

The next major breakthroughs in carp fishing were to revolve mainly around tackle and terminal rigs.

Reels were to move forward from Mitchell 300s and 410s on to ABU Cardinal 55s and 57s and then on to Shimano Baitrunners, which are still mainly the vogue today. Rods excelled, whether they were made from fibreglass or carbon – which was

proving to be a much more responsive material as well as being much lighter in weight and generally nicer to use. Lines were being made more reliable, hooks were made

> **The hair rig is possibly the biggest breakthrough carp fishing has seen**

sharper by a chemical process. Now, there is a big lesson to be learnt at this point – which is that no matter how good your tackle is and immaterial of what bait you are using and how you are presenting it, it is what is going on inside your head when you are fishing that brings success.

Where were we? Terminal rigs. During the late 1970s, some forward-thinking anglers were beginning to realise that it might be possible that those cunning carp could be picking up and ejecting our hook baits without us knowing anything about it, let alone putting them on the bank.

Also, one thing that had always been difficult was actually hooking the carp in the first place, due to our hooks being buried inside the baits being used. This was magnified even further when fishing at long range with baits such as boilies.

So was born the hair rig. The 'hair', as it is known, is perhaps the biggest breakthrough that carp fishing has seen. Even today, some 20 years later, the hair rig and its many variations are still the most popular and effective rigs to use when people fish for carp.

The main reason for its effectiveness is that the hook is exposed, which means the fish are much easier to hook, and indeed do hook themselves in many instances.

'Unethical' some anglers called it, but in mine and most people's minds it was a fine bit of trickery that took a lot of the hard work away from carp fishing.

Tackle and bait was now advancing at an incredible rate. Bite alarms were produced that were reliable and didn't play up in the wet. Special rod stands known as rod pods made fishing on hard banks a whole lot easier. Bivouacs and comfortable bedchairs made overnight fishing a lot nicer, and ready-made boilies could be bought off the shelves of most fishing tackle shops.

It was now very easy for most anglers to equip themselves properly and to go out standing a very good chance of catching a carp – which by now were becoming a lot bigger and more widespread.

Various specialist carp fishing organisations were being formed, such as the Carp Anglers Association (which is no longer about) and the Carp Society.

Anglers could go along to regional meetings and conferences, and watch talks and slide shows presented by the top carp anglers and could meet them to share ideas.

Specialist carp magazines were coming onto the scene, and many more informative books on the subject were appearing on the book shelves.

Into the 1990s and the record would be toppled once more, firstly by a spawn-bound fish which was caught twice in a very short space of time by carp anglers Roddy Porter and Alex White in the old closed-season when it was first abolished; and then by carp-catching genius Terry Hearn, with the legendary carp known as 'Mary', from the equally legendary water, Wraysbury pit, in Berkshire.

Today carp fishing is very big business and there are an awful lot of very large carp out there to fish for.

In essence though, carp fishing is not very different to the days when Walker first cast his line into the mysterious depths of Redmire – except that we now have a lot more equipment and bait with which to fish. In fact, the choice and range available is so wide that a newcomer to the sport can get very confused!

'Mum, is there any chance of buying me this Farstrike carp rod in the Bennetts catalogue?' That was my request back in

A new record

On 16 June 1980, using old-style tackle and sweetcorn, *Passion for Angling* star Chris Yates was to set the carp angling world alight. Chris set a new British record with a 51lb specimen from Redmire Pool. The small pool, locked away in the Herefordshire hills had done it again. This fish was to set the standard all hardened carp anglers wanted to break. Carp fishing entered a new era.

1970, when I was just 13 years old. The answer was 'Yes', and I fished with that rod, as well as with various others, for bits and pieces for an entire year without catching a single carp.

Now read on through these pages to find out how to use that rod and tackle like it properly, so that you will stand a better chance than I did, back then. Who knows, you might even catch a carp or two!

Rods, reels and bite indication

Getting the basics correct is more important than having the most expensive fishing gear

The mention of carp fishing might conjure up the image of a glum-looking angler, wearing camouflage gear behind a space-age set-up doing nothing. Or you might picture a proud angler slipping a specimen carp carefully back into the depths. This might inspire you to go and buy loads of equipment, so you can be just like him. But to the carp it doesn't make an iota of difference what you look like.

▼ *A baitrunner would be Lee's number one choice for a carp fisher's first reel.*

The truth is, however, that having the right set-up for the kind of venue you want to fish will help you catch more fish. This is due to a number of factors, including being able to cast to the right spot, hook more fish and play them with confidence.

In this chapter I'm going to run through what I consider to be the correct tools for the job, and in doing so will cover the full price range so that you can make up your own mind as to how extravagant you wish to be in your pursuit of carp.

Before I go on I'd just like to make the point that expensive tackle is generally more expensive because it is of better quality or is made from pricier materials. But at no time should it be misconstrued that it will necessarily catch more fish. It is the angler using the rod and bait and the spot to which it has been cast that brings success.

In a nutshell, carp can easily be landed on match rods, poles and even fly rods. However, what none of these rods are capable of doing is coping with modern-day end tackle or dealing with carp in weedy or snaggy conditions when fishing for bigger fish. Nowadays, there is a vast range of carp rods available, most of which are up to the job in hand. The ideal length for a carp rod is 11ft-12ft, a 12ft rod being more suited to casting further.

You'll notice that carp rods are usually sold with different test curve ratings, 1.5lb, 2lb, 2.5lb and so on, which means the amount of weight needed to pull the tip round so that it is at 90 degrees to the butt. Usually, the optimum casting weight for a carp rod is approximately one ounce per one pound test curve. For example, a 2.5lb test curve rod is best with a 2.5oz weight.

This does not mean that it will not be able to deal with lighter leads or leads that are slightly heavier – it's just that the casting performance will be better.

To be successful in carp fishing you need to be able to present your bait where it gives the best chance of catching. If you are out fishing on a large water this 'best chance' could be 20 yards from the bank, or perhaps even 80 yards out.

For this reason, I think the ideal test curve for an all-round carp rod is somewhere in the region of 2.5lb-2.75lb.

▲ *A bait cast to the right spot is way, way more important than having every piece of carp kit that's on the market.*

You could go heavier still to get more casting distance, but you will then come up against the problem that the rod has not got enough 'give'. Therefore there will be more chance of losing a carp due to line breakages or the hook pulling out when you are playing it close in under the rod tip.

◄ *A fixed spool reel with a large capacity spool is better for larger waters, where a longer cast is required.*

So what dictates the price of a carp rod? The material it's made from is the main governing factor, plus the quality of the rod rings and fittings used for their makeup.

> I could probably have caught a lot of the carp that I've ever landed using a set of £40 carbon/glass carp rods

Fibreglass is used for the cheaper ranges of carp rod, which usually sell for between £30 to £50. Somewhat nicer is carbon fibre which, although more expensive, at around £60 to £140, is of stronger construction than fibreglass. Because carbon is a lot lighter and more responsive, carbon-fibre rods tend to be more suited to the stresses and strains of modern-day carp fishing.

The next stage are carbon rods that incorporate kevlar-type materials in their make-up. Kevlar –a material used in the construction of Formula One racing cars, as well as being used a lot in the aerospace

▼ *Modern-day, electronic bite alarms will alert you to a taking carp.*

industry – is an extremely lightweight, yet strong material. When used in fishing rod construction, it produces a very light rod that is highly impact resistant, making it less likely to break should you bash a tree with it. It's also less liable to breakage when overloaded. In other words you can cast a heavier weight and, should you have to contend with a large fish in difficult circumstances like weed or snags, the rod should stand up to the job.

Rod rings and fittings are also a governing factor as far as price is concerned. The Japanese company Fuji is, in my opinion, the world leader in rod rings and fittings. The quality of product that Fuji produces is second to none. In carp rod construction there are two main types of Fuji ring, namely those with high-grade aluminium oxide inserts and the more expensive silicone carbide (SIC) versions.

Both types are extremely long lasting and of extremely good quality, unlike the copycat versions that, in my experience, are prone to damage and to having their centres fall out!

It's important when purchasing a carp rod that you inspect the rings in detail before parting with your hard-earned cash. There's nothing worse than losing a big carp because the centre of a ring has fallen out and the line worn to breaking point.

So what do I use? Well to be perfectly honest, I could probably have caught a lot of the carp that I have ever landed using a set of our 'Tackle Box' £40 carbon/glass 'Carp Stick' carp rods, but instead, at the moment I'm using a set of 12ft, 2.75lb test curve Century Composite NGs that cost around £200 each.

I choose these because I fish large

waters, which means I need a rod capable of casting long-range if required. I also need a rod capable of dealing with a powerful fish that is thrashing around in the margins at 2 a.m. as I'm trying to net it.

Because I fish waters that hold big fish I need to have 100 percent reliability in the kit I use. It would be pointless me spending three nights a week fishing for these bigger fish if the kit I was using couldn't land them.

Due to the speed and violence of a taking carp, it's important to have your reel set in a manner that will yield line easily in readiness for a bite. Failure to do this could result in a lost rod and reel as the hooked fish speeds far away across the lake!

With ordinary reels this means either fishing with an open bale arm, a loosened clutch, or setting the anti-reverse in the 'off' position so that the reel's handle can spin backwards. None of these options are perfect, however, as the occasional tangle can and will occur. For this reason a reel with a built-in 'Baitrunner' facility is undoubtedly the best choice for carp fishing.

Baitrunner reels have levers at the back that ,when engaged, will put the spool in a 'free running' position. This enables the reel to yield line smoothly and efficiently and a small turn of the reel's handle will disengage the lever, leaving you to play your carp by whatever means you choose – backwind or clutch.

Undoubtedly the leaders in the field of Baitrunner technology are the Japanese companies Shimano and Daiwa. As for the best models to choose, with Shimano it is the 6000 or 8000 Nexus models and with Daiwa the Regal-X 4050 BRT Bite 'n' Run.

Both companies offer more expensive models, such as the 6000 or 8000 GTE or the Emblem-X 4550 BRIT . These have more ball

bearings and are therefore smoother and will last quite a bit longer.

Any of these reels will be perfect for most carp fishing situations.

For some reason or other, waters nowadays have become weedier and weedier, which necessitates the use of higher-breaking strains of mainline.

Because this is thicker in diameter it drastically cuts down on casting distances and for this reason a lot of today's carp anglers have moved over to what have become known as 'Big Pit' reels. These reels were initially designed and manufactured for sea fishing but are now accepted as a normal sized reel for carp fishing.

No doubt about it though, they are the tools to use on big, weedy waters where you need to use heavy breaking strain lines of

around 15lb or so. Initially, anglers using these reels would loosen the clutch so that the reel would yield line in the event of a run. Fairly soon though, some bright spark came up with a Baitrunner conversion that can be screwed onto the front of the spool in place of the drag knob.

Although not as efficient as proper Baitrunners, because of the need to manually operate a lever as opposed to just turning the reel's handle, these conversions are a definite improvement on loosening the clutch.

The reels I use fall into the big pit category. They are Shimano 6000GT Power Aeros with our own conversions on the front. These conversions work rather like the clutch of a car, in that you pull out a central lever which compresses a strong spring in the centre of the conversion, which then allows the spool to revolve freely. It sounds

▲ A higher test curve will get you greater casting distance, but you still need a progressive action when playing fish under the rod tip.

complicated, but is fairly self-explanatory when you see it.

For me, these reels are the perfect size for modern-day carp fishing and because of their sensible line capacity, there is no need for any backing line in order to fill the reel up.

Recently, Shimano came up with a new Big Baitrunner 'Long Cast' reel, which is a big-pit reel with the baitrunner facility built in. I also use a set of Shimano Baitrunner M reels. Summing up though, ordinary-sized baitrunner reels are adequate for most carp fishing situations, and would be my number one choice for someone planning to buy a first carp reel.

▲ *Rod pods are great for stability and for hard banks, but Lee actually prefers single banksticks.*

So what is needed to rest the rod and reel set-up on? For most circumstances ordinary extending banksticks will be adequate and, although not essential, it is best to have your rod or rods set up so that they are somewhere nearly parallel to the water's surface.

This will ensure that your reel gives line more smoothly in the event of a bite. Two banksticks will therefore be needed per rod, one of which the butt of the rod rests on and the other which should be positioned somewhere near the butt ring of the rod.

For fishing on harder ground where it is difficult to push banksticks in, or fishing on concrete banks or wooden platforms, special rod stands called rod pods can be purchased. Indeed, some carp anglers like to use a pod all of the time because it makes for a neater set-up. There is a wide variety of different rod pods available, although at the end of the day they serve basically the same purpose. But it has to be said that some are more stable than others.

There is a growing trend towards stainless-steel pods and sticks in the modern carp fisher's armoury. The cheaper versions are fairly basic and, because they don't generally have adjustable legs or banksticks, they are sometimes a bit limited in their use. The more expensive stainless-steel pods are a lot more versatile. They are fully adjustable and generally a lot neater to fold away. Companies like Solar Tackle specialise in this type of pod and these will be the best buy in the loing run for an angler intending to use a pod all the time.

If you intend carp fishing with more than one rod, and especially if you intend to use a pod, you will need what are known as buzzer bars. These screw into the pod or into any bankstick that has got a female thread on the top, and enable up to three rods to be fished at a time without the fuss of messing about with two banksticks per rod.

Four-rod buzzer bars are also available, but these really are a specialist bit of kit, intended mainly for anglers fishing abroad.

A little tip when buying buzzer bars. Always buy a slightly wider bar for the front as this ensures that your rods splay out nicely as well as giving a bit more space for your reels. An inch or two difference between the two bars is about right.

For the back rest or rear buzzer bar you will need screw-in butt rests on which to rest your rod. These are fairly inexpensive items that all do basically the same job, so there is no advantage in buying the more expensive versions.

▲ *A bobbin is used as a visual indicator.*

For the front rest or buzzer bar, you will need screw-in rests that allow the line to run freely through them, or a better option is to have an electronic bite alarm. This is a useful bit of kit that will alert you to a bite, as well as enabling you to take your eyes off your rod to scan the water.

Having said all that, I actually prefer to use single banksticks to support my rods. I do this because I find a pod rather restricting when I want to fish two or three rods in different directions. Using single banksticks I can set up my rods a short distance from each other and have them pointing in various different directions.

▲ *You can now get a range of effective bite alarms from as little as £20.*

Most of today's bite alarms are fairly reliable and are a far cry from the older versions, which would often play up in the wet.

Possibly the best known and most reliable alarms are those that are made by Fox International and Delkim. The one drawback with Delkim is that although their alarms are excellent, they don't produce any cheaper versions, whereas Fox produce alarms that are extremely good, easy to use, and sell for as little as £20. A good example is the Micron M alarm.

The bite alarm is purely an audible aid to alert you to the fact that a fish has picked up the line and is running away or towards you with the bait.

Most alarms work on the principle of a wheel, which the line is drawn over as a fish moves off with the bait. As the wheel rotates it acts as a circuit breaker and causes the alarm to sound.

Besides using an alarm you could also consider using a visual indicator, to tell you which way the fish is running. This is called a bobbin. When a fish moves away from the rod tip the bobbin will rise. If a fish moves towards the rod tip the bobbin will drop.

The simplest and normally cheapest form of bobbins are the hanging types such as the Solar 'Danglers' or the Fox 'Hangers'. These are suspended under your bite alarm by a length of cord or chain. A very visual head is attached to the other end of this, and then clips onto your line between the alarm and your reel.

These types of bobbin, like most others, will show up all types of bite whether it be a tiny 'lift', a full-blooded run, or what is known as a 'drop back' bite, which may occur if a carp has picked up your bait and then swims back towards you.

Another quite common type of indicator is the 'Swinger' type. These work in exactly the same way as the hanging type, except that instead of a cord or chain, they have a stiff wire to which the indicator head is attached. Swingers also have a moveable weight, which can be slid along the length of the wire in order to alter the tension or combat drag.

You can do the same thing with the hanger type of bobbin, because these usually come with add-on weights that screw or fix on below the head.

Yet another type of indicator is the 'Springer' which is similar to the hanging type except that a flexible fibreglass arm is used, which resembles a quivertip.

This type of indicator is especially useful if you are fishing at long distance and wish to keep your line as tight as possible to your terminal tackle in order to show up the bites. Sometimes, and especially if this type of indicator is used at closer range, bites will be extremely violent because they offer a lot more resistance to the end tackle.

One final thing with indicators is that all of them can normally be fitted with night lights or betalights to enable them to be seen clearly when fishing at night. You usually just slip the night light into a special slot.

I use the Solar danglers, to which I can attach additional weights to combat the tow if I need to. I find them easy to use and they offer me a good, reliable form of visual indication in both day and night, as they are fitted with betalight night lights.

Finding your fish

Taking your time is the key here – look for the right spot, and only then start fishing

Undoubtedly the most important factor when getting to your chosen water is the selection of the swim. Unless you have fished the water before and have a fairly good idea of where you should fish (and even then preconceived ideas can often end in failure), do take your time when choosing where to fish.

Spend a bit of time looking round in search of those important signs, such as rolling and leaping fish, and bubbling and clouding up of the water, which will be more apparent if the water being fished is fairly clear. Pay particular attention to weed and

lily beds. If the carp are there, they should betray their presence if you look hard and long enough.

Reed beds are another place to look. If the carp are in amongst these, then the reed stems will normally 'twitch' as the carp brush through them, although this can also be caused by smaller species such as tench and bream, so a visual sighting is a bonus.

One essential bit of kit is a pair of good-quality polarised sunglasses, which will cut out the glare of the water, enabling you to see a lot more clearly into the depths. It's surprising how much more you can see with

them. In fact, I'd rate my sunglasses as one of the most important bits of kit I carry.

Look at the direction if there is any wind. It's not always the case, but carp on many waters will often be found at the windward end. Study the weather forecast before you go. Although it may be calm when you first get to the water, it may be that the wind is going to get up later on, in which case you can set up in readiness for its arrival and hopefully, arrival of the carp.

As a rule, summer carp get up early, so despite the discomfort of dragging yourself out of bed at some unearthly hour, try to do likewise. Be there when it matters, because by the time that the majority of the country is on its way to work, the best time to catch high-summer carp might already have passed.

If there are any other anglers on the water, without making a nuisance of yourself, have a little chat. Find out if they have seen any signs of fish, and find out if anything has been caught recently. Any little clue that you get might be an important factor as to whether you are successful or not.

Chances are, you'll probably get it all wrong the first couple of times you go to a water, especially if it's new to you. Don't let this get you down though, because you won't

◄ *Always set up your net first, because you just might catch a carp on the first cast.*

▲ *Time spent walking around the fishery spotting where the carp are will help you catch.*

get put in prison if you don't succeed in catching a carp.

Most carp anglers, myself included, get it all wrong most times they go fishing. It's learning from these mistakes that will teach you the right way to go, eventually.

Once you have chosen your swim, there is no need to rush straight in there. Have a little recce around the lake whilst setting up your landing net – you never know, you might be needing it fairly quickly if you've made the right swim choice!

Just a little point on landing nets. A landing net suitable for landing large species such as carp should have arms that are at least 36 inches long (42 inches is the norm) plus a handle of between five and six feet. Anything smaller than this and you will struggle to land your fish, especially if you are trying to do it alone, and you could end up losing a fish because of it.

Next, get a rod set up and baited, ready to go. I do this at home and most modern-day rod holdalls and slings are designed to carry rods in this state. This obviously saves a lot of time when you get to the water, which is particularly important if you intend to stay only for a short session.

Other items of tackle such as banksticks, rod pods, bite alarms and so on can be forgotten for the moment, as they are not yet needed at this stage. Often for the first hour or so of my sessions, I leave all my gear loaded on the old barrow, apart from the rods, just in case I see anything elsewhere and therefore need to make a move quickly. Once you are all set up and have all of the kit out of the bag you are sometimes a bit loath to move swim. Then along comes Joe Bloggs and plonks himself down where you should have moved to but couldn't be bothered, and wallop! he catches a lunking great carp. Are you gutted, or what?

It doesn't really matter what your set-up looks like, as this will not catch more fish. It's where you cast the bait that is the key factor, so again, don't be in a rush.

What I generally do, unless I am certain I have made the right choice of swim in the first place, is cast out the rods and then lay them on the bank by the water's edge. If you

▲ *Strong arm line clips.*

do this you must ensure that your reel can yield line freely, otherwise you could lose the whole lot if you get an early bite. At other times, my brain refuses to let me cast out at all unless I see signs of a fish.

I can remember on one occasion walking a total of nine miles round and round a reservoir looking for a sign of a carp. It was worth it though because I saw one eventually and five minutes later a big, fat 25-pounder was lying on the unhooking mat.

Sometimes you will have your rods already cast out and then see a carp roll or leap – and by the time you have reeled in and sorted yourself out again, you have forgotten exactly where it was that the fish showed.

If a spare rod was ready to go, however, an accurate cast could have put your bait in the circle left on the surface by the rolling fish, and then you know that you are in the money!

Right, let's now assume that you are happy with your swim choice; so what's next? Try as much as possible not to disturb the water too much. It's all very well having

◀ *Kit yourself out with an unhooking mat and a sack. Fish care is very important.*

a swim with carp in it, but if you make a lot of disturbance then the chances are that you will spook them off before you start.

On many waters nowadays, the carp are very aware of being fished for, so any wrong moves on your part could ruin an entire day's fishing. It's all very well reading about how to use a feature finding/marker float but to use one when you already have carp in your swim can often lead to disaster. 'Carp scaring floats' is the name I have for them!

Feature finding and plumbing is best carried out when you are not actually

▼ *Once you are happy with your swim choice, get those baits in the water.*

fishing. You don't actually need to know the depth of the water or its underwater features when you can see evidence of carp in your swim. All that is needed are one or two accurate casts near to where you can see the fish. If you don't succeed in actually catching on this occasion, then you can always return at a later date with the feature-finding rod, in order to try and find out where you went wrong.

If the spots being fished are close to the bank, then it goes without saying that you should be as quiet as possible. Vibrations travel through water, therefore you should avoid stomping around the bank as much as possible and your main kit such as your

rucksack or box should be positioned as far away from the water's edge as you can get it. If you need to eat some food, get a drink from your flask. Or if you are tackling up or replenishing your hook baits, then do so quietly, without making your presence known to the carp.

Even your clothing becomes important when you are fishing close in. Now I'm not suggesting that you should get yourself dressed up as if you are going into a combat situation, but drab-coloured clothing should certainly help you to blend into the bankside surroundings a little better. This will make it just that bit harder for those plump carp to detect you.

> Try to be
> as quiet as possible
> when setting up your
> banksticks or pod

Obviously the further out from the bank you are fishing then the less things like this will matter. But when you leave home you can never be sure how far out you will be fishing, therefore you should dress accordingly before you set out. Reds and royal blues look very nice in photographs, but if the carp spot you first, you might never get the opportunity to take one and you'll be left green with envy as your mate, who is dressed like Colonel Gadaffi, happily poses with a nice double!

Once you have cast in and are happy with the positioning of your hook baits, now is the time to set up your banksticks or rod pod plus bite alarms and bobbins.

I would suggest that if you are right-handed that your rods should be positioned on the right of your swim, leaving yourself plenty of room on the left of your rods so that you can get to them easily. Obviously if you are left-handed then you should reverse this order.

Again, try to be as quiet as possible when setting up your banksticks or pod. Although it may on occasions be necessary to use a mallet in order to get your banksticks into the ground, try as much as possible to avoid it.

Although not totally necessary when setting up, your rod or rods should ideally be set up so that they are supported at the front and the back. They should either run parallel to the bank or should be angled downwards slightly towards the water. This way, bite detection will be better and more prominent. Your front rest or bite alarm should be positioned somewhere near to the butt ring of your rod and your back rest should go somewhere below your reel on the handle section of your rod.

▼ *Once you have cast out it's time to set the bobbins and wait for a bite.*

Next, clip your bobbin onto the line and, whether you are using a Dangler type hanging bobbin or a Swinger type, this should clip on between your reel and the butt ring of your rod.

Although not essential, many carp anglers like to use some sort of line clip directly above the reel. I use the Solar Tackle Strong Arm Clips, although there are other good versions available from Fox International and Gardner Tackle.

These line clips usually grab the slack line, enabling you to set the Baitrunner setting or clutch fairly loose without the possibility of line being able to come off the reel due to drag on the line. Another advantage with line clips is that once you have cast into position, you can really tighten up to your lead and then 'clip up' to keep your line as tight as possible.

By doing this you will be offering a lot more resistance to your end tackle, which will give you a better 'bolt rig' effect. When the carp sucks up your bait there will be a far greater chance of your hook pricking its mouth, therefore causing it to bolt off.

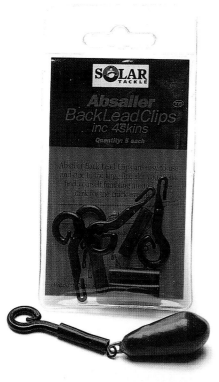

▲ Sit near to your rods so you are able to react to a bite quickly.

Beware though – bites when fishing clipped up can be very violent and will often take you by surprise; so be ready!

All of this said, carp on some waters will often be very wary of tight lines running parallel through the water and so will avoid the area at all costs. In this instance it will be more beneficial either to fish with slacker line or to use what is known as a back lead. You clip this onto your line beyond your rod tip after casting out, thus pinning your line down to the lake bed and out of harm's (or rather, fin's) way.

There are no hard and fast rules with this one, however, so you need to experiment a little to see what is best on your water.

So that's about it really; all you now need to do is wait for that run. Other important items of tackle, such as an unhooking mat and your landing net should be positioned in the best places possible. In the case of the net, this should be within easy reach to enable you to land your carp. Your mat needs to be in a nice, flat position away from the water's edge and out of the way of any dangerous obstacles that could cause

possible damage to the carp, should it choose to misbehave a bit once on the bank.

Your own positioning should be as close to your rods as possible, which is particularly important if you are casting near to snags or weed, so that you can be on the rods quickly and steer the fish away from the danger areas such as snags and weed beds.

If you are using an umbrella or bivvy, set this up a bit further back, leaving yourself plenty of room to manoeuvre at the front of the swim for playing a fish.

Whilst waiting for a bite, some carp anglers like to read a book; others like to catch up on some sleep after a manic week at work. Me? I'd like to do both of these but instead I'm usually running round the lake like a mad thing, looking for the next bite in readiness to load up the old Carp Porter and move swims!

Phew! I think I might be getting a little bit too old for all of this...

Carp baits

A look at sweetcorn, worms, meat, maggots, bread ready-made boilies and frozen baits

Sweetcorn

As far as carp and a lot of other types of fish are concerned, that Jolly Green Giant has got a lot to answer for, because due to their liking for him, he has caused them an awful lot of uncomfortable excursions to dry land. Sweetcorn is a bait I like very much and in its time it has been responsible for some massive catches. It will catch from the outset, but I do find it beneficial to prebait a few spots beforehand with corn in order to attract the fish and keep them coming back for more. Three or four pouchfulls is all that is required in each spot although before now I have used a couple of catering tins of the stuff in a single day session, such is the carp's liking for the stuff.

When using corn as a hook bait I would nearly always suggest fishing it on a hair rig, mainly because if you don't it is possible to get what is known as a 'bite-off'. This occurs when the carp are feeding heavily on the bait and the hook bait gets passed back beyond the carp's throat (pharyngeal) teeth, and the hooklink gets bitten off. As with meat, flavoured and coloured sweetcorn is also available and can be effective, due to being a little different. Personally though, I like those lovely little natural golden grains, which is how they're intended.

STEP-BY-STEP: HAIR RIGGING SWEETCORN

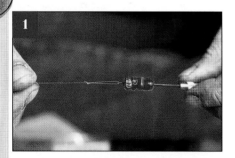

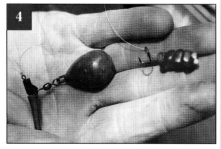

1 Use a baiting needle to thread four grains of corn onto the hair rig.
2 Once the grains are in place, trap them in place with a hair stop.

3 The grains of corn should sit on the hair in a position, just off the hook.
4 The finished rig is presented with a semi-fixed bolt rig, like this.

Worms

Call me a heretic, but in my opinion worms are very overrated as a bait for carp. This is only a personal opinion because obviously carp have been caught on them in the past. All I ever seem to be able to catch on them, however, are perch and eels, and when I have tried worms for stalking carp it's as if those carp are oblivious to them, whereas they'll snaffle up maggots with gay abandon. Other anglers I know have had some results when using worm, but the carp tend to be on the smaller size. Chopped worm is becoming a popular bait for smaller carp on commercial fisheries, fed with casters with a whole dendrabaena fished overdepth over the top.

There are a number of other natural baits that can be used for carp, such as swan mussels or even water snails. But I think it might be illegal to use swan mussels now and although all of these types of bait will have their day, for modern-day carp fishing using natural baits, in my opinion, maggots and casters win hands down!

Meat

Although I don't use meat a great deal nowadays for my own fishing, it is a very versatile bait that will catch extremely well on most carp waters as well as being an excellent bait for other species, such as barbel and chub.

Most brands of meat that you see on the supermarket shelves will be suitable as bait, although you will find that some have a firmer texture than others, so are more suitable as bait. When I used to use meat a lot, I found that the varieties containing casein or caseinate in their makeup were the best, so it's worth scanning the ingredients on the side of the tin before making your purchase, to see if either of these is included.

Funnily enough, to me, the firmer varieties never seemed to taste as nice as the sloppy ones, which reduced the inclination to eat my bait should I get peckish during a session. Another alternative to luncheon meat is a product named Bacon Grill, which is a similar sort of thing but is a lot greasier and seems a bit more effective at catching fish. Meat is good bait on silty or weedy lake beds because it's reasonably buoyant, so will not disappear from sight very easily and will remain detectable by the fish.

One little dodge is to cut up a few hook bait-sized cubes and microwave them for two or three minutes. Once cool, these cubes are very tough

STEP-BY-STEP: HAIR RIGGED MEAT

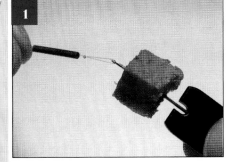

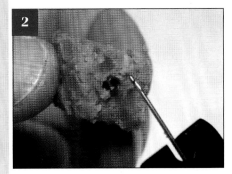

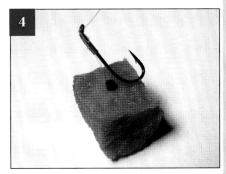

1 Thread the meat and silicone insert tube onto the hair like this.
2 The tube insert is used to stop the meat splitting on the cast.

3 In the loop on the hair use a stop made from a small length of twig.
4 The meat should sit in position like this, just off the shank of the hook.

and more suited to fishing on rigs such as the hair rig. Be careful though ,and be sure to check before casting out, because this cooking process sometimes causes the meat to float: great if you want to try it for surface fishing or fishing as a

pop-up, but not much use if you wish to fish it on the bottom. As well as ordinary meat, a number of companies such as Van Den Eynde and Sensas produce specially flavoured varieties such as strawberry, trout pellet and mussel and shrimp.

Frozen baits

Freezer baits do not contain preservatives and will therefore go off after two or three days if not used up. I would not advise re-freezing them as they never seem as effective. It's the same as with human foods really: it shouldn't be re-frozen otherwise it will cause you an upset stomach, so why not the same for fish? One little short cut to help you decide what variety to use is to ask about successful flavours on the waters that you intend fishing or ask at the local tackle shop. They will have a fairly good idea of what is being used by knowing what is selling best. It generally seems to follow that what is being thrown in the most, will be the best bait to choose

as the fish will often view this as a form of natural food, and will not view it with as much caution.

If you are unable to find out what is being used, then as a rough guideline, I would suggest a fishmeal-based variety for summer and autumn, examples of these being Richworth's Crab and Mussel, Mainlines Activ 8, Kevin Nash's Squid mix boilies or Nutrabaits Big Fish Mix ready-mades, to name just a few.

For winter and spring use I would steer clear of the fishmeals and go towards the bird food or 50/50 mix varieties such as Rod Hutchinson's Chocolate Malt or Mulberry Florentine, Mainline's Grange CSL or Essential Opals, Nutrabait's Pineapple and Banana, Nashy's Big Strawberry Birdfoods or my own personal favourite, which is

Richworth's Tutti-Frutti freezer baits, closely followed by their Pineapple Hawaiian variety. Whatever you choose, you can rest assured that the ready-mades you will be using have been specially formulated with the sole intention of helping you to catch carp, as well as taking away the inconvenience and guesswork of making your own!

Maggots

In this age of modern-day carp baits such as boilies, it can be easy to forget that carp still consume much natural food during their everyday lives. Often to the extent that at certain periods of the year they show a distinct preference for this over any other type of food. For this reason, natural-type carp baits can prove to be winners. My all-time favourite is red or white maggots. When using maggots I prefer to use a mixture of live and dead ones, because if the live ones bury themselves in the lake bed, there will still be the dead ones left to attract the carp. To kill the maggots I seal them in a polythene bag and then pop them into the freezer for a few days before use.

When it comes to baiting up with maggots, if the distance being fished is close in, they can be catapulted easily or thrown in by hand. But for getting them further, other methods will be needed. One way is to use a product known as 'Sticky Mag' which is available in most tackle shops. Another method is to 'spod' them out using a bait rocket, such as Gardner Tackle's dinky little 'Pocket Rocket' which is perfect for the job and can easily be cast using any carp rod, so there is no need for a specialist spod rod. There are no rules as to the amount of maggots to groundbait with. As a guide, I would suggest putting out a pint to start with and seeing how it goes. Obviously

STEP-BY-STEP: HAIR RIGGING MAGGOTS

1 Light line, hooks, maggots and a needle are needed for threading maggots.

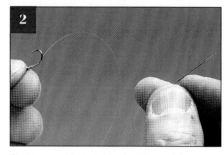

2 Use an eight inch length of line and tie one end to the eye of the hook. Thread needle on other.

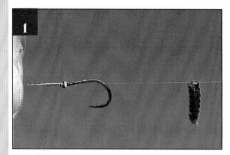

1 One by one thread the maggots onto the line with the needle until you have enough.

2 Wrap the line around the shank of the hook to create a ball of maggots, and tie off loose end.

species other than carp will also show an interest. This can be a good thing because any fish feeding on your baited patch should help to attract the carp in. For the hook bait, using an ordinary sewing needle I thread 20 or so maggots onto a length of low-breaking strain line. Once I have done this I tie the length of line to either the bend or eye of the hook. You can use small hairs of

maggots or, if you prefer, wrap the length of line with the maggots on around the hook. Another clever way of presenting maggots is to fish them 'popped-up' on a rig known as the 'Medusa' rig. Superglue as many maggots as you can onto a half-inch polystyrene ball and then using a boilie baiting needle, present it on a hair rig in much the same way as a boilie.

Ready-made boilies

It wasn't all that many years ago that all of the baits used for carp fishing had to be dug up out of the garden, bought from a supermarket, or made up yourself. Nowadays we are almost spoilt for choice as ready-made boilies are available in many different sizes and varieties from all of the major bait companies, throughout the country. Ready-mades are available in two different forms: the 'shelf-life' varieties that contain preservatives in order to stop them from going off, or the 'freezer-bait' varieties.

One question that I'm often asked is how long do shelf-life boilies last once you have opened the

packet. The answer to this is indefinitely, provided that they are stored correctly. The main thing is keeping the baits dry and free from condensation.

What I would always suggest is that once the bag is open, tip them into a brown paper bag (the sort that you get from a greengrocer) or a small cardboard box. This way, should they get damp in any way, then all the moisture should be absorbed by the paper or cardboard. Obviously, if you intend to use up your bag of boilies fairly quickly then this doesn't matter and they can be left in the bag that they came in.

So how do you choose what variety to use? This is an impossible question to answer because every single variety of ready-made boilie has

probably been well tried and tested, and does and will catch carp.

My own personal preference, however, is for the freezer-bait varieties because it is my belief that for most forms of fishing, fresh bait is best. I'm sure that the preservatives used in shelf life, albeit in small quantities, can be detected by the fish and that they don't like them very much.

To give an example of this as a comparison, crush up a tiny Bob Martin tablet and then mix it in with a tin of your dog's favourite dog food. Result: the dog won't eat it! That said, however, the resident dog on the water that I mainly fish, 'Bruce' the rottbrador, eats absolutely anything: contact lenses, tea bags, sunglasses, beer cans and even frogs. In fact nothing is safe when 'King Rat' is on the prowl for food.

Bread

Perhaps one of the most underused and underrated baits for catching carp is that old favourite, bread! In this age of high-tech tackle and boilies, baits like bread are often overlooked. Yet without a shadow of doubt, it still remains one of the most versatile baits ever.

Bread as a bait has caught literally thousands of carp in the past and no doubt will do so in the future. The thing is, it is a bait that most carp in all waters have seen and enjoyed eating before. After all, there's always someone feeding the ducks, geese and swans with bread, so you can bet your life that there are a few carp swimming about below, mopping up the leftovers. Perhaps one of the main reasons that many anglers steer away from bread is because it is very vulnerable to falling off the hook. But it's not a bait for fishing a long way out, anyway.

My favourite time for using bread is when stalking, in which case it doesn't need to stay on the hook for a long period. With this type of fishing you are generally creeping round with one rod and recasting fairly regularly.

Often, when carp can be seen milling around in mid-water, a large piece of breadflake taken from the centre of a fresh loaf, pinched onto the hook and then freelined in amongst them, can be a mouthful that even the wiliest carp finds extremely hard to resist.

The thing is, when presented like this with no additional weights attached, the flake generally sinks fairly slowly and wafts enticingly about as it does so, therefore behaving like no other bait can. Another devastating way of using bread is to use it floating on the surface: floating crust in other words.

The main difference between using flake and crust is that crust is best used from a stale loaf as opposed to a fresh one. The main reason for this is that it will be tougher, and therefore less likely to fall off the hook when casting. Another method I have used to good effect is to combine the two.

Often with floating crust, the carp will swirl near to it and because the crust gets waterlogged it will break up and bits will be intercepted as they drop from it. What I do is pass my hook right through a fairly large piece of crust and then pinch a piece of flake onto it. As the carp swirls, the bread breaks up and bits drop from it, along with the piece of flake to which the hook is attached.

This is a devastating method that will work on most waters if you are given the opportunity to try it. This was the method that accounted for my one-time personal best of just under 29lb, which I caught back in 1978. Although there are very few methods of fishing with bread, it's something that can be made a little

▼ *Good old bread, catcher of many a carp.*

▲ *Make your own bread and flavour it with milkshake powder.*

different by baking your own. Why not try making a loaf from one of the home-make bread mixes that are available in most supermarkets? Then you can go on to make the bread a little different by adding some flavouring before baking it in the oven.

An old favourite of mine (when I could keep from eating it myself) was to stir in some banana-flavoured milkshake powder to the bread mix. The permutations that you can go on to try with the home-baking routine must be endless.

Carp absolutely loved the banana flavour and it was something that often worked when the carp completely ignored ordinary bread. So, next time you see those carp swimming aimlessly around on the surface and all other baits are failing dismally, get the old sandwiches out and try a piece of bread that has got some added taste and flavour. You might be pleasantly surprised.

Mainlines and hook links

These items of terminal tackle are your lifeline to catching those carp

Terminal tackle is a major part of the carp angler's armoury, and making the right choice can mean the difference between a fish on the bank or another blank.

It's all very well having a good set of tackle, but what is perhaps more important are the less expensive items. These items are the lifeline that determines whether or not you land a hooked carp, or indeed if you hook one in the first place.

So let's start with what is the most important item of all, mainline. The thing to determine most are the waters where you intend fishing. Obviously if they are weedy or snaggy then you will need to up your breaking strain a little in order to stand a greater chance of landing your quarry.

Or if they are relatively snag and weed free, then you will be able to get away with a lower breaking strain of line.

So why not use a high breaking strain of about 15lb all of the time?

Well the thing is, the thinner the diameter of the line that you use, then the further and easier you will be able to cast, which is an aspect to consider if the carp on your water appear to be a long way out from the bank.

Personally, I fish a number of different waters where from one minute to the next I am never totally sure whether I will be fishing in the margins or casting to the horizon. Therefore I compromise, and use a 12lb breaking strain line for most of my own carp fishing. I do, however, sometimes use braided mainline which, because of its low diameter in relation to its high breaking strain, is excellent for long-distance casting and for playing fish in weedy or snaggy situations. I'll come to that later though.

Most 12lb breaking strains will be suitable for the job, although I would suggest going for one of the well-known makes as most of the time these have been thoroughly tried and tested.

▲ *Gold Label's Pro Gold and Sufix*
Supreme are both reliable brands of line.

Brands of line that spring immediately to mind, although I must apologise to any well-known line manufacturer that I miss out, are Gold Label's Pro Gold, Sufix Supreme or Synergy, Fox Soft Steel, Gardner GR60 which is a favourite of carp supremo Terry Hearn, Berkley Big Game or XT and the inexpensive Daiwa Sensor or the new Technium line from Shimano, which is a bit of a cross between monofilament and braid, hence its expensive price tag.

So let's say you've bought your 12lb line. How do you get the best from it? One of the most important things is loading your reels correctly. Now there are a lot of different schools of thought as to how you should do this in order to avoid annoying line twist. Personally, I find the best way is to poke a pencil through the centre hole of your bulk spool of line, get another person to hold either side of the pencil to keep the line under some tension and then wind it onto your reel, making sure to apply a steady tension as you go.

▼ *With such a wide range of terminal tackle, lines and hook lengths to choose from it's important to make the right choice.*

Your spools should be filled to about an eighth of an inch of the spool's lip, in order for you to be able to cast to your optimum performance.

For extreme long-range carp fishing and when conditions dictate – in other words, when the water being fished is relatively weed and snag free – dropping down to a lower breaking strain and thinner line diameter will add yards to the distance that you can cast.

One thing that is necessary if you do this, however, is to use what is known as a shock leader, in order to take the initial brunt of the cast. A mono shock leader is fitted to ensure your mainline doesn't break, a 'snap off' as it is termed.

Shock leaders should be in the region of 25ft long and to be safe should have a breaking strain of between 15lb and 20lb.

The one unfortunate thing about using leaders though, is that it is another knot in your

line, therefore a weak point if you haven't tied your leader knot properly.

The knot that I use for attaching a shock leader is a double grinner knot using five turns with the mainline and three turns with the thicker leader line. Once tied and fully tightened, you should give your knot a proper testing by pulling the lines either side of it. Obviously if it breaks fairly easily, then you need to get a bit of practice at tying it properly, although if you still can't manage to tie it correctly then I'd suggest dispensing with a leader altogether and returning to using a 12lb breaking strain mainline. You'll just have to hope that those long-range carp move a little bit closer in and to within your range.

As I said earlier, braided mainlines are a real boon for long-distance casting and because of their low diameter in relation to their high breaking strain, they are ideal for long-range carping. Beware though, they are not really suited for the beginner.

The problem with braid is that unlike mono it has practically no stretch, so playing fish on it can be a hairy experience. Unless you are careful you will lose fish through hooks pulling out of the fish's mouth, or hooklink breakages.

If you still fancy giving it a go, however, the brands that I have used and can thoroughly recommend are Berkley Fireline in either 10lb or 14lb breaking strain, Rod Hutchinson's 24lb Sabrebraid, Sufix Herculine which is labelled up as 30lb breaking but has a wet knot strength of around 22lb, or 22lb Dynon SK.

Another thing to consider with braids is that in comparison to mono they are very expensive, so unless you are absolutely sure that you are going to like using it, stick to ordinary line. One plus, however, is that they do last a lot longer than mono. So although on average they cost about three times as much, they do as a rule last about three times as long. Therefore it works out about the same in the long term when it comes to cost.

One fallacy that I will dismiss with braid is that a lot of anglers worry that it will cause damage to the inside of their rod rings. This is total rubbish, as the materials that the insides of rod rings are made from are extremely hard, unless you set about them with a hacksaw.

A final few points before moving on from mainlines. Always buy lines that have been thoroughly tried and tested. Ask your tackle dealer whether he or she has tested the breaking strain. If not go to a tackle dealer who has done so.

The problem with a lot of mono lines is that the stated breaking strain on the label often bears no relationship to what the actual breaking strain of the line is.

As a rule you will find that lines of similar diameter break at a very similar breaking strain, therefore one line manufacturer might label his 0.35mm diameter line as 12lb breaking strain whereas another might label it as 15lb!

At the risk of having court proceedings being brought against me, it's a bit of a con really, and there is no one being conned more than the money-spending public. In match fishing circles it is rife and if only these anglers were to do a few bench tests on some of the lines that they are buying then they would find that all is often not quite the same as the advertising blurb states.

▲ The right hook link material can make a huge difference to how many bites you get.

Avoid at all costs monofilaments that have been pre-stretched as these are next to useless for hard-pulling fish such as carp. Although they will cast extremely well, you will find that they snap like cotton when faced with the sudden lunges of a hard-fighting fish. I'll climb down off my soap box now and move on to hooklink materials.

As with most forms of fishing, that short bit of material to which your hook is attached can make so much difference as to how many bites you get. In match fishing the increase in bites when dropping from say a 4lb hooklength down to a 2lb hooklength can be quite incredible. Well, it's exactly the same in carp fishing except that you obviously wouldn't go down that low.

Many years ago I can remember an old angler saying to me: 'See them bubbles out there lad? Them bubbles are caused by the fish laughing because they can see your line, so are therefore eating all of your free bait but ignoring your hook bait!'

Well, I believe the old chap wasn't quite right, in that I don't believe that it was the sight of the mainline that was putting them off, but more the fact that the hook bait was tethered to a thick bit of line. So it was behaving unnaturally and completely differently to the free bait.

In carp fishing there are now so many different types and brands of hooklink materials available that it can become extremely confusing, especially to the newcomer. Hopefully I will dismiss some of the confusion, although it must be understood that sometimes even the most experienced carp anglers have to scratch their heads with regard as to what to use. Even then they will often get it wrong, especially when deciding what length of link to use.

My favourite hooklink material is ordinary monofilament, the reason being that nowadays it is different to what the majority are using, therefore can offer a bit of an edge. Also, one of my pet hates is tangles and mono is far less prone to tangling than dacron or most of the various braids. In my mind there is nothing worse than sitting behind a couple of carp rods wondering whether or not my end tackle arrangement is resembling the aftermath of grandma knitting a couple of pairs of socks and a woolly

jumper at the same time!

As with monofilament used for mainlines, I would again recommend choosing one of the tried and tested brands. My particular favourites are Gold Label's Pro Gold or Berkley XT (extra tough) if only for the reason that they tie up nicely and lie along the bottom well.

The decision as to what breaking strain to choose really depends on the water being fished. As the old man was trying to state, the finer you go, the more bites you will get. You can't be silly though: obviously you need to be using a breaking strain that offers you more than an average chance of landing a hooked carp.

As a guideline I would suggest a breaking strain of 8lb if the water being fished is relatively snag and weed free, 10lb if there are a few snags and a bit of weed about, or 15lb breaking strain (14lb is the nearest to this in Berkley XT) if there is a lot of weed

▲ *With balanced tackle, mainline and hooklength, Lee places the bait in the target area.*

and snags. For most of my hooklinks the knots I tie are a five-turn twice through the eye grinner knot for the swivel end and the knotless hook knot for the hook end.

Another hooklink material that is becoming very popular amongst carp anglers are the fluorocarbons. These resemble monofilament in appearance, except that they are usually clear in colour and have what is termed 'similar light refraction qualities' to water. Basically this means that they are less visible in water than normal monofilaments.

Personally though, I don't think that visibility comes into it very much when fishing on the bottom for carp, especially in the middle of the night! That said though, fluorocarbons are undoubtedly less visible to the human eye, so they might be worth a try when fishing with a popped-up hook bait

where a certain amount of your hooklink is sticking up off the bottom, or for fishing on the surface.

There are a number of different fluorocarbons now available and the makes that I have tried with some success are Sufix Invisiline and Korda's new 'IQ'; which isn't to say that the others are not very good, because undoubtedly they are.

The one thing that I do find with fluorocarbons is that they don't seem quite as tough as ordinary mono and are also a little bit unreliable on knot strength.

For this reason I'll stick with ordinary nylon for most of my own fishing. Most of the time I'm fishing for that one bite in a blue moon and the biggest carp in the land, so I cannot afford to be using tackle that I'm not 100 percent confident in.

When fishing more prolific waters with a good head of smaller fish you can afford to experiment a little. So don't write off some of the things that I don't suggest.

A lot of people reading this will never have seen dacron, as it is no longer available in many tackle shops. Basically, it is a material that is made from polyester and, because of its limpness, it makes a good hooklink material for carp fishing. One problem with dacron though is that it is not terribly abrasion-resistant, which is one of the reasons why it has been superseded by the modern-day braids. Braid is available in a whole variety of colours and breaking strains. Braid is probably the most popular hooklink material used nowadays although, as I said, I personally don't use it a great deal because of the problem with tangles.

Despite there being a lot of different makes of braid available, in reality there is very little to choose between them all, although some do seem a little more supple than others. They also have different buoyancies, which means that some float, some sink and some have a sort of neutral buoyancy, and hover somewhere in between.

As far as I know, all braids are made of kevlar-type materials and because of this are extremely fine in diameter for their breaking

▲ *Perfect presentation of both bait and terminal tackle will put fish on the bank.*

strain and very abrasion-resistant, which is ideal for fishing on snaggy waters.

Kryston Products produce the biggest range of braids and were as far as I know the first company to bring them out back in the 1980s when a brand called 'Silkworm' was introduced. Kryston's range is now so big that it can be a little difficult to know which to choose. All I can say to help you make your choice is that my favourite in the range

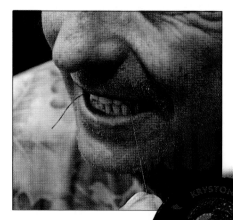

▲ *One way to strip off the outer coating of Snake-Bite!*

is 14lb Supersilk, as it is the supplest of the lot, as well as being very tough and very fine in diameter. If you need to use a higher breaking strain, then 25lb Silkworm would be my choice.

If you want to use a lower strain then 8lb Merlin would be my choice. A lot of other manufacturers produce braids for hooklinks – namely Drennan ESP 'Sinklink', Mainline 'Mainlink', Richworth 'Sorcerer' or Rod Hutchinson's 'Edge' range to name just a few. In short I cannot be of very much help to you here, because in reality I cannot find very much to choose between any of them. Whatever you choose you should be happy with, because they are all excellent.

Another type of hooklink that you hear about now and again are 'Stiff Links'. These, as far as I know, were the brain child of former Carp Society chairman Mike Kavanagh and the reason behind their effectiveness is reckoned to be that they are hard to eject once the carp has sucked in the hook bait.

A variety of different

'Braid is probably the most popular hooklink material used today, although it tangles.'

materials can be used to form a stiff link, as basically all that they are is a length of heavy, thick line about four to six inches long. The most popular materials for this are a special memory-free fly fishing line called 'Amnesia' in 20lb breaking strain or the very versatile Kryston 'Snake-Bite' material in 25lb strain. Amnesia is very much the same as ordinary monofilament, although it does seem to behave a bit better and does not kink very easily.

Snake-Bite, on the other hand, is a bit more complex and has a braid as the inner material, with a stiff plastic-type outer coating. With Snake-Bite there are numerous ways that it can be used and there are a lot of different suggestions, with instructions in the packet when you buy it.

Personally, if I ever use it, which has been quite a lot of late, I prefer to strip off about two or three inches of the outer plastic coating at the hook end of my hooklink, so that my bait behaves more naturally. Then, because the rest of the link is stiff, I still get a good stiff link effect, plus hardly any tangles.

I'm not sure if there is a correct way of stripping the outer but I strip it off between my teeth, although if you do this you must ensure you spit out and discard the plastic coating – you don't want to swallow it!

At the swivel end of a stiff hooklink, it is generally more effective to have a loop as opposed to an ordinary knot. This gives the link more freedom of movement and means that the bait is more likely to enter the mouth of the carp no matter what position the fish sucks at it from.

This loop is formed by tying a simple overhand knot, remembering to put the swivel onto the hooklink material before proceeding to tie it. The length of hooklink to use is at times a little difficult to decide, as there is no ideal or correct length. The perfect length to use can vary from day to day.

Longer hooklinks, of say 18 to 36 inches, will offer a more natural bait presentation, although this will also give the fish more room to manoeuvre, and therefore more chance of ejecting your hook bait. Short links of say four to ten inches on the other hand, although not giving as good a bait presentation, do ensure that you get a better 'bolt rig' effect from your end tackle. The fish comes up against the resistance of your lead weight very quickly which can lead to self-hooking.

Another thing to consider when deciding what length of hooklink to use is what you are fishing on – in other words, what's on the lake bed.

If you think or find that the lake bed is very silty or if there is a covering of bottom weed such as silkweed, then it is best to use a longish hooklink, so that your hook bait remains detectable above it.

If you are fishing in holes in the weed or up against snags, the reverse will be best, because you want your hook bait in close proximity to your lead and not tethered somewhere up above. If the water being fished is neither silty nor weedy, then you can afford to experiment a little.

If two rods are in use then it may be better to start off with one rod with a short hooklink and the other with a long one and see how you get on. However, don't take it for granted that what works best one day will necessarily work best the next, because carp fishing is very rarely as cut and dried as that.

In comparison to those of humans, carp have relatively small brains, but they do learn by association. Therefore, if everyone fished for them with 10-inch hooklinks, then they would fairly quickly suss it out and the person who went in with something different would probably clean up. With end tackle for carp there is only one rule and that is that there are no rules. Keep ringing the changes to try and keep one step ahead of both the fish and the other anglers on your water.

▼ *Just some of the hooklength materials Lee has used.*

Leads, hooks, swivels, rig-tube and beads

All these items have a place in the carp fisher's armoury

A lead is a lead isn't it? All it's used for is to cast the required distance, right? To a degree I'd agree, but in reality the major carp lead manufacturers such as Korda and Essential Products wouldn't go to all of the trouble they do to produce the different shapes of leads if they didn't think that leads had a place in a carp angler's armoury. After all, the guys behind these companies are experienced carp anglers themselves. They haven't come up with a different shape of lead just for a gimmick. It's derived from a need within their own carp fishing.

Basically, carp leads are produced in two different forms: what are called 'in-liners', and the type that have either a swivel or a wire loop protruding from the top of them. I call these 'hang on the side' leads.

Both types have a place in carp fishing, therefore it's worthwhile carrying a selection of each in your tackle box. The main differences between the two is that the 'hang on the side' leads will cast a bit further, especially the more aerodynamically-shaped ones such as the Korda distance with swivel.

They are also generally a little bit better for 'feeling' for features with, which is vitally important if you are drawing back your end tackle in order for it to rest against a weed

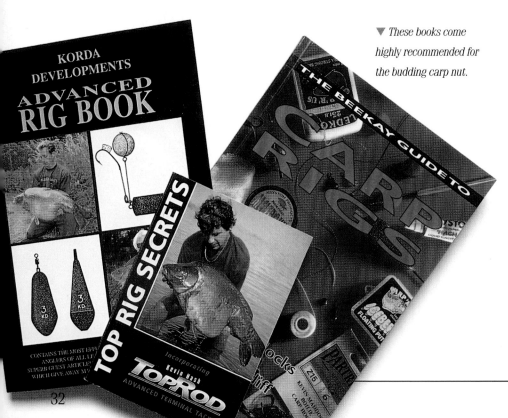

▼ These books come highly recommended for the budding carp nut.

bed or a gravel bar, or if you are using a marker float set-up.

In-line leads offer a more streamlined and neater set-up. Furthermore, they are just that little bit less prone to tangles. These are the main two reasons why the majority of carp anglers choose to use them.

The 'hang on the side' leads are either used directly on your mainline, with the line going through the swivel, or they are attached either to a link swivel or to a special clip such as the Kevin Nash Safety Bolt rig clip. In-line leads on the other hand usually have a length of plastic tubing running through their centre and are attached by passing your mainline through the tube and then into what's called a 'semi-fixed' position.

When I say semi-fixed I'm refering to the fact that the lead is held in position on a tube that fits snugly into the central core. However, should a fish break the line, the lead will in fact be able to work its way off the tube and the fish can rid itself of the lead and tubing.

As for the many different shapes and sizes that leads come in, these can be categorised into three main groups which are: aerodynamically shaped ones for long distance casting; dumpy-shaped ones to give a better bolt rig effect, and flat-sided ones that not only give a good bolt rig effect but also sink more slowly through the water and are therefore more suited to fishing on soft, silty lake beds and over bottom weed.

Flat-sided leads are also very suitable for fishing on the slopes of gravel bars and plateaus etc – because of their shape, they shouldn't roll out of place.

Before moving on I'd better explain this 'bolt rig' effect business. Basically, most of today's rigs involve the use of 'exposed' hooks, which is the case when using any form of hair rig.

The idea is that the hook's point should 'prick' the carp's lip when it either picks up or ejects your hook bait. This happens because it meets resistance from the weight which is fitted to the rig in a semi-fixed style. The hook pricking the carp makes the fish bolt off in blind panic. The outcome of this is hopefully a steaming run at the indicator end of your set-up, and the shorter your hooklength is, the better the bolt rig effect will be. This is why you see so many carp anglers using seemingly crude six-inch hooklengths.

It all sounds a bit complicated but I can't think of a simpler explanation.

▼ *Lee shows some of his preferred terminal tackle.*

HOW A BOLT RIG WORKS

As the carp picks up the bait the hooklength is brought into contact with the weight of the lead. This causes the carp to bolt away from the lead which in turn pulls the hook home

The carp picks up the bait on a slack hooklength. As it starts to move away the 'bolt' effect comes into play

For maximum bolt rig effect a 3oz Korda lead is used and is fitted to the line with a Nash safety clip

As I have already mentioned when talking about carp rods, generally the optimum lead in order for the rod to perform at its best is one ounce per one pound of the rod's test curve. In other words a 2.5lb test curve rod will generally perform at its best with a 2.5oz lead. This is not to say that you should always use a lead of this size, but it is a good starting point, and one that only experience will tell you when to stray from.

From my own point of view, although complicating matters a little, I prefer to use fairly light leads of around 1.5oz to 2oz despite the fact that for most of my carp fishing I use rods with a 2.75lb test curve. This really comes about because I like to be using something a little bit different to what most people are using. I do this in order to try to trick the carp a little, and if you were to analyse what is the most popular size of lead carp anglers buy, then you'd find that it is either 2.5oz or 3oz.

Don't forget, I work in a tackle shop that specialises in carp fishing equipment and bait, therefore I get to notice these little things. That said though, there are times when I'm slinging a 4oz lead as far as I possibly can towards the horizon so, like I said, there really are no hard and fast rules when it comes to lead sizes.

Along with line, which I covered in the last chapter, hooks are another item of end tackle that cannot be skimped. Hooks need to be reliable in every possible way, if you are to stand a more than reasonable chance of landing a hooked carp, or even hooking one in the first place.

Fortunately, nowadays there are many good patterns of purpose-made carp hooks available that are all up to the job, a far cry from not so many years ago when it was necessary to check every hook in the packet and discard any that didn't come up to scratch.

Take a look at the diagram above, which should explain the whole bolt rig process a little better.

Now, the more compact a lead is in relation to its weight, the greater the resistance that will be transmitted to the hook. Therefore, dumpy pear leads or round ball-shaped leads will be more efficient than the more elongated versions.

To explain this another way, think about picking up a 3oz ball as opposed to a 3oz stick. Although they both really weigh the same, the ball will actually feel a little heavier because its weight is more condensed – get it?

As for the weight of lead to use, there are no hard and fast rules as to which is best for the job.

▲ Lee favours size 6 hooks for most of his fishing.

Quality control seems to be a lot better now though, and you rarely come across any imperfections, which is just as well really, because hooks are no longer a cheap item of tackle.

Perhaps the most important feature is sharpness, because there is no doubt about it, the sharper the hook, the more fish you will hook in the first place.

Most hooks nowadays are sharpened using a special chemical process which gives a much sharper point as a result. But because of this, they are a lot more prone to point damage, especially when fishing on waters with gravel bars and snags etc.

▶ Lee's personal preference is for a hook actually designed for trout fishing

Personally I tie on new hooks at the start of every session and then check the points for sharpness again before every

cast. If I find that it's not quite as sharp as it should be, then I have no hesitation in changing it. I never try to re-sharpen a

hook because, no matter how hard I try, this usually results in it ending up even blunter.

Hook strength is the next thing to look at, although most modern-day carp hooks are more than strong enough for most carp fishing situations. The only exception to this might be if you are fishing in extremely weedy and snaggy situations, in which case the thicker-wired, stronger patterns should be used.

It's very difficult for me to recommend actual patterns to use because, as I said before, the majority of modern-day hooks are very good. Hook choice is also a bit of a personal thing. One top carp angler's choice might vary from another's, yet at the end of the day they will both be successful at catching carp.

If pressed, I'd say that my preference is for a pattern that is not even designed for carp fishing. Instead I use a pattern intended for trout – the Kamasan B175 lure hook. These hooks are extremely sharp, relatively light in weight and fairly strong. And what's more, because of their long shank and in-turned eye, they offer excellent hooking capabilities for carp fishing.

The size I use most is a size six, although I do sometimes scale down to an eight in the winter, when the carp tend to be a bit more finicky. On average, I'd say that a size six hook is a good all-rounder to choose, immaterial of what pattern of hook you are using or the type of hook bait you have chosen.

Perhaps the only times that I would stray from this size are when fishing on the surface, in which case I would probably choose one of my other favourite hooks, a size eight Drennan 'Super Specialist', or when fishing abroad. Then I'd go up to a size four or even a two if I was fishing with a multiple boilie set-up – two or three boilies on a hair rig at the same time. The reason for this is that a lot of the carp in foreign waters will never have been hooked before, so they fight like stink, because they think that they're being taken home for dinner.

So what other patterns of good carp hooks are available? Well, the answer is loads, and although I will stick with my B175s for the moment, because I'm happy and confident in them, I'd probably be equally happy with the hooks from Fox, Nash, Mainline, Gardner, Drennan, ESP, Gold Label or Partridge, to name just a few.

Also, a lot of these companies produce barbless versions which is handy on waters where barbed hooks are banned.

◄ *The use of the right terminal tackle combined with a perfectly presented bait was the downfall of this stunning carp.*

One final thing on hooks before moving on. Most of the time for my own fishing I tie on my hooks using something known as 'the knotless knot' (see page 52 for step-by-step instructions). The knot involves the hair rig being a continuation of whatever hooklink material you are using. Once mastered, the knotless knot is an excellent way of presenting your hook bait and is very simple to tie, thus cutting out the need for the novice to have to pay over the top and buy ready-tied hair rigs.

So what other tackle bits and pieces are there that I consider to be really the absolute necessities?

Firstly, swivels are essential in order to attach your hooklink and mainline.

My preference is for the flat-sided swivels known as rolling swivels. These come in a number of different sizes in order to fit the various rig components and leads available. The sizes of most use for carp fishing can be anything from a size seven to a size 11, which is about the smallest that you are ever going to need. To give an example of why you may need a number of different sizes, a size 11 fits perfectly into a Kevin Nash safety bolt rig clip, which is a rig component that I often use. A size eight fits nice and snugly into the insert of a Korda in-line lead, which is another popular choice amongst carp anglers.

Although they may not appear to be strong enough, even the smallest of these swivels (the size 11) will have enough strength to land any carp that swims. So there is no need for you to worry on this count.

Anti-tangle tubing is an important part of your end tackle in that, as the name suggests, it helps to cut down on tangles. Not only this, it also offers a bit of extra protection to your end tackle when fishing over gravel bars. And it offers protection to the carps' flanks when you are playing them, because it is far less likely to lift scales than monofilament when your mainline comes up against the side of a fish during the fight, which is something that always happens. Anti-tangle tubing threads onto your mainline above your hooklength, swivel and lead, and in order to cut down on tangles as much as possible it needs to be longer than the length of your hooklength. Although it comes in a number of different bore sizes, I would suggest that the best size to buy is 0.75mm, as this will fit into most rig components, such as tail rubbers, tulip beads or things like Solar Buffer Beads.

You will notice if you have browsed through any carp-tackle catalogues that there are a number of different makes available. Whatever you choose to buy, whether it be Nash No-Spook, Solar Quick Sink, Korda Camo or the Gold Label stuff, all of them will be good enough for the job. There are a couple of makes available that are a little bit different, namely Kevin Nash Mussel Cracker tubing and E.S.P. Anchor rig tube.

The Nash stuff is reinforced with kevlar, therefore it's a lot more abrasion resistant than normal tubing and is best suited for fishing over gravel bars or where there are mussel beds about.

The Anchor tube is a lot heavier than all other tubings, therefore it is useful if you wish to pin down your end tackle to the lake bed.

As well as leads, hooks, swivels and anti-tangle tubing, there are a variety of other useful end tackle bits and pieces, such as snap links for clipping your leads onto, rig rings for making a free-running set-up, the previously mentioned tail rubbers as well as a variety of different beads that can come in handy.

Rather than go into these now, I'm going to leave this until the next chapter, where I'll explain how to set up a number of different rigs as well as explaining how to mount your baits. There will be lots of easy to follow photos and diagrams to help you along.

Rig construction and mounting baits

Carp rigs for you to make and use

Now it's time to move on to the construction of end tackle. We're going to take a look at how to put together some of the more popular carp-fishing rigs and look in detail at the components needed to make these rigs.

There are now hundreds of new hooklength materials, hooks and rig building components, so it's important to pick the right kit for the fishing situation you are faced with.

Just because a big-name angler catches a large fish from a water and the rig used is shown in the press, it doesn't mean that the same rig will catch fish on your own water. It's a case of horses for courses, and you must get it right.

What I hope to do over the next few pages is to take the guesswork out of rig making and leave you with no doubt as to how to make the rig of your choice with ease. Once you have a better understanding of your own water, you will get to know what sort of presentation is needed to catch the resident carp.

When you draw that hooked carp over the rim of your landing net, on a rig that you've made yourself, there's a great feeling of satisfaction and it is also a great boost to your confidence. Remember, don't complicate things – at the end of the day it is often the simple rig that works best.

In case you've forgotten, the running rig involves the use of your lead weight running freely on your mainline, therefore offering little resistance to the carp once it has sucked in your hook bait. There are no hard and fast rules as to when this rig is best used. Being very simple and easy to set up, it's an arrangement that is ideal for those of you who don't want to mess about too much or clutter your end tackle with too many bits and pieces. The simplest running rig set-up, and perhaps the one most commonly used, involves threading your mainline through the swivel that is mounted in the top of your lead weight. Then you thread on a bead – for example a John Roberts or Solar Buffer Bead – to act as a shock buffer and knot protector, before tying your mainline onto the hooklength swivel. However, as time moves on, you may want to

adapt this rig and make it work for you as a bolt rig. The bolt effect can be achieved by simply placing a rubber float stop on to the line first, before threading on any other item of terminal tackle. Once the stop is in place, thread on a bead followed by the lead and then another bead. Then the hooklength is tied on. The rubber stop can be positioned closer to, or further away from the swivel, as required. The closer it is, the quicker the carp comes into contact with the bait and is pricked by the hook, causing it to bolt.

For fishing in weedy conditions, or if you want to make your set up even more free running, instead of having your mainline running through the swivel on the lead, a large plastic ring known as a 'low-resistance run ring' can be used instead.

These rings have a small protruding bit on the bottom which has a hole in it. This hole enables a snap link to be attached, onto which you can clip

STEP-BY-STEP: RUNNING BOLT RIG

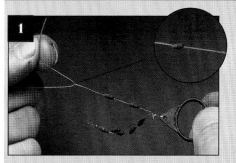

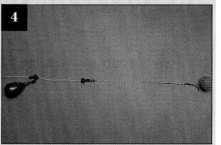

1 Thread one large rubber float stop onto the mainline as shown.
2 Now thread on a rubber shock bead and follow this with the lead and a second bead.

3 Tie on the hooklength and select a position for the rubber float stop.
4 As a carp straightens the rig by moving the bait, it comes into contact with the lead.

STEP-BY-STEP: LOW-RESISTANCE RUNNING RIG

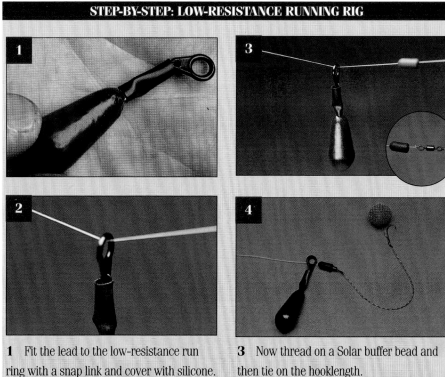

1 Fit the lead to the low-resistance run ring with a snap link and cover with silicone.
2 Once fitted, thread the lead on to the mainline as shown.

3 Now thread on a Solar buffer bead and then tie on the hooklength.
4 Draw the buffer bead down over the eye of the swivel and you are ready to cast.

your lead weight. Obviously a much larger diameter shock bead needs to be used in order to stop the ring from running over the hooklength swivel and down to your hook. Other perhaps neater types of bead to use for this purpose are either a Solar Bullet Buffer Bead, which as the name suggests is bullet shaped, or another type of bead known as a Tulip Bead, which is shaped like a tulip.

One disadvantage with this set-up is that the hooklength is prone to tangling and could sometimes be a problem, especially when using a braided hooklength material. For this reason it can be worth incorporating some 0.75mm anti-tangle tubing which should be threaded onto your mainline above your hooklength. However, you need to ensure that the length of tubing used is longer than that of your hooklength as this will stop the tangles occurring. The tube will also help protect your line if fishing over gravel bars.

Incorporating anti-tangle tubing with an in-line set-up is a little more complicated, although not too difficult to set up. Most in-line leads, especially the Korda range, have stiff plastic tubing protruding from the top of them. Now this is where a neat little rig component known as a 'Tail Rubber' comes into its own. The ones I use are made by two companies, Korda and Solar Tackle, and are tapered pieces of rubber about one inch long. They have a large bore at the fatter end and a smaller bore at the thin end. What you do with them is this: the fat end pushes over the plastic tubing protruding from the lead and you then have to gently twist your anti-tangle tubing (which again should be approximately 0.75mm bore), into the thin end of the Tail Rubber. If you have difficulty getting the tubing to fit then all that you need to do is to moisten the end of it with saliva. When buying tube don't forget to make sure it's the right size

STEP-BY-STEP: FLAT PEAR IN-LINE RIG

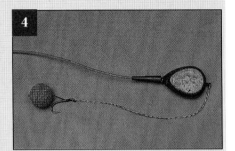

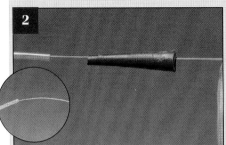

1 To construct the in-line rig you need some rig tube, tail rubber and in-line lead.
2 Thread the length of tube on to your mainline and then thread on the tail rubber, as shown.

3 Select the lead and thread this on to the mainline so the stem slips into the rubber.
4 Tie on the hooklength and pull the rubber down over the lead stem to lock it in place.

ANCHOR TUBE IN-LINE RIG

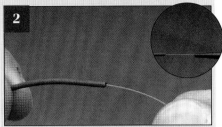

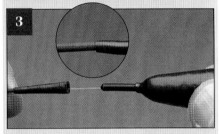

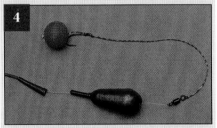

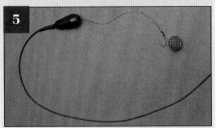

1 You need an in-line lead, tail rubber, hooklength and a pack of Anchor rig tube.
2 Cut and thread a length of rig tube making sure it is longer than the hooklength.
3 Now thread on the tail rubber followed by the lead you you are going to use.
4 Now it's time to tie on the hooklength to the end of the mainline which exits the lead.
5 Slide the tail rubber over the lead stem and then pull the swivel into the lead.

and that it fits into your tail rubbers. Although I personally never bother, some anglers choose to glue their tubing into the Tail Rubber to hold it tightly in place. You shouldn't have to do this, as most are a tight fit and this saves messing around with glue.

It may be that the carp you are after are spooking away from the mainline around the rig area. In this case I would suggest that you think about pinning the rig down on the bottom to hide the line. This can be achieved by using a weighted rig tube, behind the lead. This will ensure the line

directly behind the lead is pinned down tight to the lake bottom and that the carp don't see it. There are a few ways to do this. One is to use a length of lead core which involves splicing this to the mainline. The other is to incorporate the use of a weighted tube.

The rig that I use for the bulk of my carp fishing I call the 'hang-on-the-side-rig'. It's a form of semi-fixed rig because the lead is able to break free from the safety clip in the event of a snag. It's simple to construct and easy to cast. The rig offers me a 'bolt rig' presentation. Once the carp sucks in the bait and moves away from the lead, it comes into contact with the resistance of the weight, and pricks itself on the hook. This causes the carp to bolt away and the hook is pulled home. The lead is held in place on the safety clip by the tail

STEP-BY-STEP: HANG-ON-THE-SIDE RIG

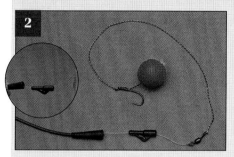

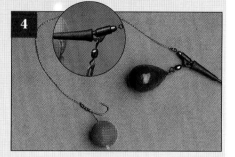

1 You need a pack of Nash safety clips, rig tube, tail rubber and a swivel bomb lead.
2 Thread tube and tail rubber, followed by the safety clip, then tie on the hooklength.

3 Now insert the swivel on the lead onto the safety clip, like this.
4 With the lead in place, pull down the tail rubber over the safety clip.

HELICOPTER RIG

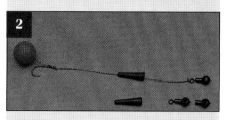

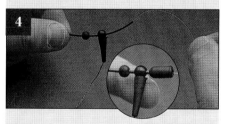

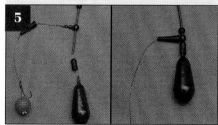

1 Most tackle shops sell ready-to-make helicopter components.
2 Tie off a short hooklength, about six inches, and include a tail rubber as shown.
3 To help thread the bead on to the mainline you can shape the tube with scissors.
4 With the mainline threaded through the rig tube add the hooklength and buffer bead.
5 Pull the top bead down to trap the hooklength in position above the lead.

◀ *As the carp lifts the bait it comes into contact with the weight which sets the hook.*

rubber on the rig tube. In the event of a break-off, the carp can rid itself of the terminal tackle with ease. The hooklength can pull free from the lead, and the mainline will exit the tube.

The helicopter rig is so called because while in flight the hooklength can be seen revolving round and round above the lead resembling a helicopter's rotor blades. This rig is perhaps the ultimate long-distance casting rig, as the lead is fished on the end of your

mainline with the hooklength fitted above it. With the lead in this position at the bottom of the rig, all the cast's power is transferred to it and great distance can be achieved. However, in my experience if the water being fished is weedy, then using a helicopter rig can lead to losing a few fish through hook pulls. This is due to the lead dangling down and catching up in the weed.

Weather influences

How to get the best results from the weather forecast

The weather has a very big bearing on how, when and where fish feed. Undoubtedly the biggest influences are wind direction and strength, temperature, air pressure and the dissolved oxygen content of the water.

Phases of the moon can make a difference too, but this is something that none of us fully understand so I won't dwell on it, other than to say that if it's a full moon and you see a werewolf roaming around your fishery, I'd stay at home if I were you!

In the UK the predominant wind direction is southwesterly and winds from this direction will generally be warmer than those that blow from the north or the east.

On most British waters these will be the best winds in which to go fishing. Carp like to be warm and comfortable in their environment, so they will be a little less comfortable if there is a chilly northeasterly blowing – as will you, of course!

You may have heard this old wives' saying: 'When the wind's in the east, the fish bite least. When the wind's in the west, the fish bite best'.

There is a lot of truth in this and it's perhaps the reason why some of these old wives make very successful anglers. When it's chilly they stay at home, and when it's warm they venture out.

Wind direction also has a great deal of influence on where natural food larders are likely to be found.

At the down-wind bank (which will be the northeast corner if a southwesterly is blowing) the surface water is pushed into it and then goes the opposite way underneath the surface. This is what's called undertow (see diagram below).

If there is a decent undertow, food will naturally accumulate not too far out from the down-wind bank, which is why fishing with the wind in your face is a very good proposition. So to add all this together, if you are in the northeast corner during or just after a warm southwesterly blow, and fish on

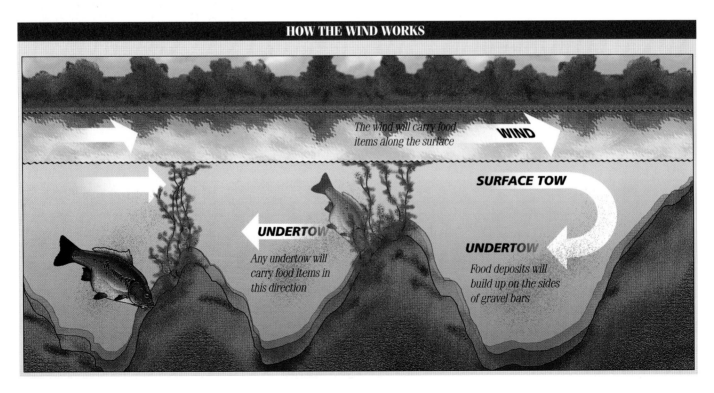

HOW THE WIND WORKS

The wind will carry food items along the surface

WIND

SURFACE TOW

UNDERTOW

UNDERTOW

Any undertow will carry food items in this direction

Food deposits will build up on the sides of gravel bars

the bottom not too far out, there should be some fish there.

Undertows on gravel pits are a little more difficult to predict – if there are a lot of gravel bars and drop-offs present, the natural food areas can be found in a number of different areas, any distance from the bank.

Depending on how near to the surface a gravel bar comes, you can get an undertow from much the same way as if it were the windward bank. Also, as the surface water pushes across it, an area of slack water will form at its base on the opposite side.

Feature finding on gravel pits can be very important, because building up a picture of how the bars run and at what height they rise from the lake bed gives you some idea as to where the natural feeding spots are likely to be in any given conditions.

A ir pressure is another strong influence on how well carp feed, although as with wind direction and everything else that Mother Nature throws at us, there are no hard and fast rules.

Air pressure is measured in millibars (mb), and pressures of 1000mb and below are considered as low, whereas pressures of 1010mb and above are considered as high.

From a fishing point of view, low pressure normally brings cloud cover and often rain and wind. The water gets oxygenated and the fish often feed as a result. I'm always encouraged to go fishing if an area of low pressure is moving in. So-called 'fair weather fishermen' miss out on these occasions, which is just as well sometimes, because it means more room on the bank for those who have donned waterproof and windproof clothing and are out there having a go.

Temperature also has a very big bearing

▶ *Spending time with a marker float will unlock the features in your lake.*

on where the carp are found. On warm sunny days carp will normally be found in upper layers that have been warmed by the sun. Therefore a bait fished on the top of a gravel bar will often intercept the carp, more so if there is a nice wind blowing to oxygenate the water.

On hot, calm days, carp will often be in a bit of a lazy mood and may be found basking about in the weed or sheltering in the shade of an overhanging bush or tree. On such occasions they will be ever so difficult to tempt, with perhaps the only good chance

being if you use surface-fished baits such as Chum Mixers or bread.

I f the weather forecasters predict such conditions then get there at the crack of dawn if you can, because this might be the only opportunity you'll get of a bite until the sun starts to cool down in the evening.

Contrary to what you read, sunny days during the winter can be absolutely storming and also contrary to what is often said, it's the shallower areas that can produce rather than the deeps. Shallower water gets

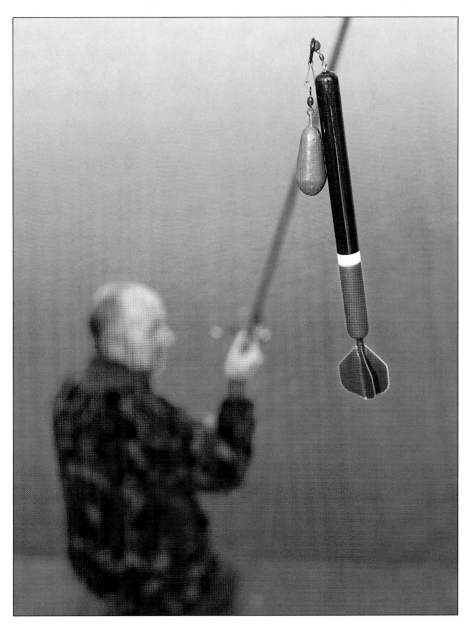

▲ Hit the mark, hit the fish!

▼ Once you have built up a map of your lake all the depths and features can be added in as you find them.

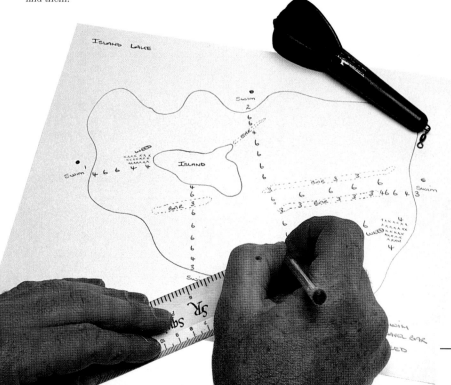

warmed more by the sun and gets oxygenated by the wind, so this is where the carp will like it best.

If I were planning a winter campaign for carp fishing, then my ideal water would be relatively shallow. In this case the carp will respond quicker to changing weather conditions and be on the lookout for food when the weather is favourable.

What about rain? Normally it rains during periods of low air pressure, therefore it will generally be a good time to get a bite or two.

My favourite times are when you get a sudden heavy downpour on an otherwise fairly sultry day. Again the oxygenation of the

HOW A MARKER FLOAT WORKS

When surveying the bottom of the lake, you will need to drag the float one foot at a time across the bottom to establish the correct depths. If you only take one reading and fish to this mark you may be missing a better feature to the left or right of the *original mark. Once you have dragged the float forward, allow it to rise to the surface and take a reading. Do the same thing every time you drag the float and you will get a true vision of the bottom area you are fishing over.*

water really gets them going and searching for food.

Thunderstorms? Wow! The lull before and after, or right in the eye of the storm are stunningly productive times for a bite, although I must admit to feeling a little bit nervous about playing a carp using a carbon rod when lightning is striking.

Continual rain I dislike. I'm not exactly sure why, but during periods of continual rain it seems that fish can be put off the feed.

Hand in hand with the weather comes feature finding. You may have noticed that I have made a number of references to water depths when talking about the weather. Indeed the knowledge of how to use a feature finding/depth finding float can be absolutely invaluable – see the diagram above.

As a rule you can gauge the depth of water that you are fishing in by 'feeling' your lead down through the water and then feeling for the satisfying 'donk' as your lead

goes down and strikes the lake bed.

'Easier said than done' I hear you say, and you'd be right, because this action takes a lot of practice to perfect.

What you need to do is this: at the point at which your lead weight hits the water's surface, draw your rod tip upwards and then allow your lead to sink to the bottom on a tight line. When the lead hits the bottom, the rod tip will bounce back. In effect it's like lowering your lead through the water in much the same way as you do when sea fishing from a boat.

Once perfected, this procedure can give you all sorts of useful information, such as how deep the water is, what the lake bed is like (whether it is soft and silty or hard) or whether or not your end tackle has landed in weed, in which case your hook bait could be hidden from detection by the fish.

Feature finding is best carried out when you are not actually fishing because the disturbance caused can often be a bit counterproductive to fishing, plus you can

concentrate better on the job in hand if you haven't got to worry about setting all the gear up and baiting up.

Also, take into consideration other anglers on the water. Some of them will not take too kindly to a brightly coloured marker float being continually cast in and out of the water. I know that this is one of my own pet hates, especially if I've been settled in and fishing for a few hours.

Let's look at how to set up a feature finding float. A number of the tackle manufacturers produce purpose-made marker floats, although basically they are all very similar in that they resemble cigar-shaped pike or sea fishing floats, but have highly visual flights on to in order for them to be more stable in the air. This enables them to be cast and seen at a greater distance. For feature finding in weedy conditions, use the most buoyant float you can.

You don't particularly need any extra equipment in order to plumb and feature find, as the normal rod and reel that you fish with should suffice. The only thing that is a definite advantage when feature finding is to use a braided mainline. It's worth having a spare spool loaded with it, specifically for this purpose. Because braid has no stretch, the 'feel' that you get on your rod tip is much more positive than when using ordinary monofilament.

Setting up the float is extremely simple. Your lead weight is best attached via a snap link to a large ring such as a John Roberts Low Resistance Ring or a Solar Eazi-Glide Run Ring which is then threaded onto your mainline so that it runs freely.

Then, before tying the float on to the end of your mainline, you need to thread on quite a large bead in order to protect the knot and to stop the float from getting damaged by the lead and ring.

The procedure for plumbing is as follows. First, cast into the water, allowing your lead to hit the bottom, and then tighten up to the lead. At this point the marker float will also be on the lake bed resting up tight against the lead.

▲ *Dark clouds start to form, bringing rain and a change in the weather – will the carp bite tonight?*

Then, either by loosening the clutch of your reel or by disengaging the Baitrunner facility if your reel has one, slowly feed off line a foot at a time, in order for the float to rise to the surface.

It is worth marking the butt of your rod in some way one foot above the reel so that you can get a reasonably accurate measurement. Once you see the float bobbing to the surface, make a mental note of how many feet of line you paid off your reel – this represents the depth of the water at that point.

It's worth jotting your findings down in a notebook for future reference. This is best done by first drawing a rough sketch of what you can see on the horizon, or on the far bank. Then write down the depths in each swim as you find them.

Once you are happy that you have measured the depth fairly accurately, you then need to reel the float down to the lead once again, draw the lead and float along the lake bed for a few yards – then repeat the procedure of letting line out, again measuring the depth as you go.

Whole areas can be mapped out in this way and this is great if you want to fish with two rods in the same swim.

Obviously, with a single cast it is possible for you to measure the depths from as far as you are able to cast, right to the margins in front of you.

You can also work out bottom features as you go. By drawing your rod around parallel to the water's surface as you draw the lead along when pulling back, you should see and feel features like gravel bars or the heavy resistance that weed beds cause.

It is very difficult to describe the differences that can be seen and felt on the rod tip with the many different features that could be below the surface, but practice

STEP-BY-STEP: SETTING UP A FEATURE FINDING/MARKER FLOAT

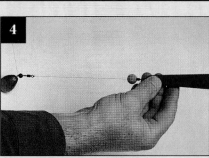

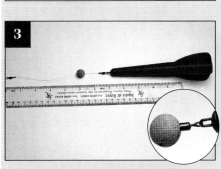

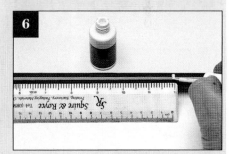

1 Here are the tools you need. A marker float, 3oz lead, a bead, a cork ball and a swivel.
2 On to your mainline thread a 3oz lead, followed by a rubber shock bead.
3 Tie your marker float to a six-inch length of line with a swivel at the other end.

4 Tie the swivel to your mainline. The cork ball will help the float rise quickly.
5 As line is paid off the reel and through the lead loop, the float will rise to the surface.
6 Mark your rod blank one foot above the reel. You can then count off the depth.

makes perfect. The more experienced you become, the better you will get at identifying what is what. Gravel normally feels like a 'tap, tap, tap' on the rod tip, although so does Canadian pond weed sometimes.

An initial heavy resistance can be felt when pulling up against a gravel bar, followed by the tap of the gravel and then the 'nothing' feel as the lead pulls off it.

Weed offers a heavy resistance all of the time, and sand, chalk, silt and clay all feel fairly smooth.

Don't worry too much if you don't think that you are getting things right because, believe you me, most of us never do get everything spot on. Indeed, it is not until you go out in a boat or if the lake is drained for some reason that you get to know what the lake bed is really like in detail.

Winning ways

The inside story of *Carp Clinic*'s competition winner

From time to time, magazines run competitions in which lucky readers can win fantastic prizes. *Improve your Coarse Fishing* ran one which involved *Carp Clinic* author Lee Jackson and in which £3000 worth of carp tackle was up for grabs. The mail bags were nearly bursting at the seams, when thousands of entries arrived in the post.

Carp Clinic fever seemed to have gripped a vast number of the magazine's readers, as the amount of entries received was staggering. But, as with any competition of this nature, there can only be one winner. So magazine carp editor Martin Ford went off to Kent and staggered around a 30-acre lake, armed with nearly 3500 competition entries, to catch up with Lee and draw a winner.

Once Martin had tracked Lee down, all the entries were tipped onto the floor of his bivvy and then it was time for the draw. In went Lee's hand and out of the mountain of entries came the envelope that was going to make one reader turn somersaults. Once drawn, the envelope was opened, and the winner was Chris Martin, from Wednesbury, West Midlands. After hatching a master plan of how the day out with the winner was going

to go, Martin hit the road back to the magazine office to make the phone call that would make Chris's day. It went something like this. 'Hello, is Chris there?'. 'No, who's calling please?' says Chris's wife. 'It's Martin Ford from *Improve Your Coarse Fishing* magazine.'

'Is it anything to do with that competition for the carp fishing gear,' she asks? 'Has he won it? I'll get him to ring you straight away! I'll just phone him at work!'

Two minutes later the phone rings and Chris is told the great news. At first there is just silence, then a great whoop of joy! Plans are set and Martin tells Chris to meet him the following week at Gold

Valley Lakes, near Aldershot, Hampshire, to collect his prize. The big day arrives and into the car park drives Chris, his wife and his best friend, who drove them down from the Midlands. Chris is told that the prize has all been set out further along the lake and that a photographer is on hand to take some pictures for the magazine. But what he didn't know was that there was a very special guest waiting for him on another part of the fishery.

On arriving at the lakeside Chris is positioned amongst his prize and a few pictures are taken for the magazine. Lee Jackson then calls Chris on Martin's mobile phone, supposedly from the Tackle Box in Kent, to congratulate him on winning the competition. As the discussion progresses, Lee asks Chris where he is and Chris replies that he's fishing on Gold Lake at Gold Valley, Hampshire. 'That's funny, so am I,' says Lee.

Chris's face turns white with shock as the one and only Lee Jackson steps out from behind the bivvy!

Now read through the next pages to follow Chris's day, as master carper Lee Jackson helps this lucky winner to sort out the mountain of carp gear and sets him off on the trail of carp, carp and more carp!

1 'Well Chris, I think the best thing we can do is go through all the items you have won and I'll answer any questions you have about them.'

2 'Before we do that though let's get the champagne out and have a toast to your win and to your first steps into proper carp fishing.'

3 'The main bait in use for carp is a boilie. There is a good selection here of ready-mades and mixes so you can make your own.'

4 'To land your carp you'll need a good sized landing net. This Relum net is just the job. As a rule the net needs to be a minimum of 38 inches.'

5 'Scales are another "must have" bit of equipment. It's no good catching a big carp and not having the right gear to weigh it on.'

6 'If you're planning on doing a few night sessions then this little cooker from Coleman is just the job for rustling up a meal.'

7 'The Colt rods you have won are both 2.75lb test curve. They are made at the Tackle Box in Kent. The reels are Shimano Baitrunner 6010s.'

8 'Time to start setting up the rods for a short session. We'll take a look at the rest of the kit later. I think you've got more kit than me now!'

9 'Before we set up I'd have a look through the rig book from Korda Tackle. There are several good rig books about at the moment.'

10 'Let's get the line threaded through all the rod rings. I'll take you through a simple but effective set-up that can be used on most waters.'

11 'This length of rig tube is used to protect the line just above the hooklength. It has to be longer than the hooklength so they don't tangle.'

12 'Once the mainline is through the tube I thread on a safety clip. This will house the lead, which is held in place by a tail rubber.'

13 'This is how it all looks when fitted together. It's a simple but safe system, and a snagged fish will be able to rid itself of this terminal tackle.'

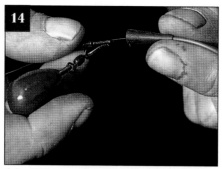

14 'This tail rubber slides over the safety clip to hold the lead in place. Now tie a hooklength and bait to the other end of the swivel.'

15 'I've got a pre-tied 6lb mono hooklength. I prefer mono hooklengths in the winter when the water is clear and the carp are harder to catch.'

16 'To tie the hook to the rig I'm using the knotless knot. So that the hair is the right size against the hook I put the bait on first.'

17 'Today I'm rigging you up with a size eight hook to which I'm going to hair rig two halves of a tutti frutti boilie.'

18 'With the rig tied and ready to go I've used some PVA string to tie some loosefeed to the rig. In winter carp won't want too much free feed.'

19 'The PVA will melt when the hook bait touches down on the bottom, leaving a neat little pile of loosefeed around the hook bait.'

20 'That's it, get the bait out there and let's get fishing. We'll soon have the bobbins bouncing once those carp find your tutti frutti boilies.'

21 'Set these '"Butt Bangers" (indicators) so that when the carp picks up the bait and moves away, the bobbin will rise, sounding the alarm.'

22 'Position the reel so the bale arm roller is at the top. This will allow an easy flow of line from the spool when the fish takes off with your bait.'

23 'Once you turn the handle on this Shimano Baitrunner reel, the reel is put back in gear and the fish is played through the drag system.'

24 'These Fox bite alarms will register a forward run with one tone and a back drop (fish moving towards you) with another tone.'

25 *'The right-hand bobbin has dropped down, and the line is peeling off the spool. Well done. Now just play him out slowly and I'll get the net.'*

26 *'The carp is trying everything to evade the net and it looks like a good fish! Gently does it, keep its head up and slowly draw it over the net.'*

27 *'That's a good fish, I reckon it's a double. Smile when you're having your picture taken, and always kneel over your unhooking mat.'*

28 *'I don't believe it, the other rod is off now. I think it's a slightly smaller fish but it looks like it's pulling a bit.'*

29 *'Get the hook out and always use a mat so the carp is protected. The barbless hook should come out easily. I think he's about 8lb, well done.'*

30 *'It's not as big as the first but still worthy of capture. Get it back into the water after a quick picture, then re-bait and get fishing again.'*

31 *'Quick Chris, one of my rods is away. Grab it and I'll get some more bait for your rod. What a session, three fish in ten minutes!'*

32 *'I'll hold the net ready under the water. Bring the fish to the net like this. If you chase it with the net you may knock it off the line.'*

33 *'Just time for a quick photo. My other rod is away now! They really have got their heads down on those tutti fruttis. Look at the mouth on that!'*

34 *'Let the rod take the strain. If you want to change the direction of the carp's run, lean the rod the other way and apply a bit of side strain.'*

35 *'Well, it's the end of the day Chris, and it's time for me to head back to Kent, as I'm fishing again tonight!'*

Carp baits

Boilies and pop-ups

The knotless knot

This sequence shows my favourite way of mounting a boilie bait. Using the knotless knot will enable you to decide on the distance between the gape of the hook and the bait. Some anglers use long hairs and others prefer short. There really are no hard and fast rules with this one, although obviously it shouldn't be too far away, otherwise the hook will not enter the carp's mouth in the first place. The top of your hook bait (the side nearest the hook) should be anything from touching the bend of the hook to about one inch away from it. The main reason that the hair rig works is because the hook is completely separate from the bait. Therefore when fishing for species like carp, whose teeth are at the back of their throat, there is a far greater chance of hooking them than there would be if the hook was buried inside the bait.

So there you have it, a few simple rigs that are easy to use and very effective at catching carp.

STEP-BY-STEP: KNOTLESS KNOT

1 Cut a 12-inch length of hooklength material and form a loop at one end.
2 Using a baiting needle, pick up the loop and thread the boilie onto the hooklength.
3 Into the loop place a bait stop. I favour the E.S.P. dumbbell stops as shown.
4 Grip the hook between finger and thumb and hold boilie in the desired position.
5 Start to wind the hooklength around the shank of the hook, trapping the boilie.
6 Wind the line down the shank about eight times and then exit, down through the eye.
7 The boilie should now be trapped in position as shown.
8 The hooklength is now ready to be tied to the mainline.

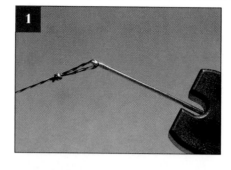

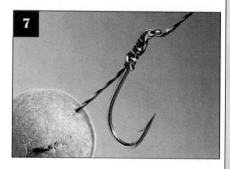

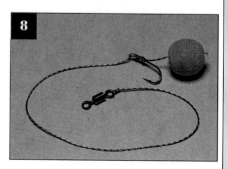

Home-made boilies

Probably the majority of carp anglers prefer to buy ready-made boilies, which is due mainly to convenience and to the amount of top-quality ready-made boilies that are now available. There is no doubt, however, that making your own can work out quite a bit cheaper. So what is needed in order to make your own? Firstly you're going to require a ready-made 'base mix', of which there are many, so you may get a little confused as to what to choose. A base mix is a mixture of dry powders (ingredients) which, when mixed with a flavour, colour and eggs, forms a paste from which boilies can be rolled and boiled. Perhaps the only guideline I can offer is to choose a fishmeal-based mix for spring and summer use or a birdfood or 50/50 type mix for autumn and winter.

Next you will require some attractors to go with the mix, and here again you may need to seek advice, although many of today's mixes have suggested recipes on the packet. The only things needed now are eggs, to bind your mix together. A little word of advice here though. Always buy fresh eggs that are well 'in date' because although you might not think so, the fish will detect the difference if you use old ones, and your bait will not be as effective. As you get more proficient at making boilies, or you feel the need to make a lot more, then this is the time to consider buying some proper boilie-making tools. A rolling table is the first thing.

These come in two sizes – either the giant-size Gardner Rollaball, which enables you to produce a lot of baits with a single sweep, or the standard-size Rollaball, which is a lot cheaper but doesn't produce as many boilies. All of these are available in a number of different sizes from 12mm up to 24mm. This enables you to produce boilies of the size of your choice. One thing that is very important when using a Rollaball is to produce the right diameter sausages, so that the baits come out perfectly round.

This can be done in one of two ways. Firstly you can roll out the sausages using a double-sided Gardner sausage table. Alternatively, the much better option is to use a sausage gun. Again, these come in different versions – the relatively cheap standard Gardner sausage gun or the more expensive professional metal bait gun. There is even one type that runs off compressed air,

STEP-BY-STEP: MAKING BOILES

1 Select your mix and liquid flavours, along with six eggs.
2 If the mix is a six-egg mix, then all the eggs should be cracked into the bowl.
3 Add to the eggs the required amount of liquid flavours.
4 Mix these together with a spoon or fork, making sure all the flavours are mixed.
5 Now start to add the dry ingredient in small quantities.
6 Use a fork to fold in the dry mix to the liquid and stir well.

7 You may find it better to use your hands to bind the mix together.
8 Once the paste has been formed, roll out sausage-shaped lengths.
9 Cut sausages into desired bait-sized pieces. An average size is 14-16 mm.
10 Each chopped bit of sausage is then hand rolled to form the boilie.
11 Take 20 to 30 at a time and boil in clean water for two minutes.
12 Allow to dry thoroughly on a tea towel and place in a plastic bag and freeze.

although because a compressor is needed in order for this to work, this really is a specialist bit of equipment and not of much use to the average boilie maker, unless of course they are feeling particularly rich. Whatever gun you choose, they all come with a variety of different nozzles that are either pre-cut or that you cut yourself in order to

produce sausages of a diameter to match your Rollaball table.

Okay, back to the kitchen and making them by hand. Take a look at the easy-to-follow sequence shown here and remember that if you don't want to use them straight away you can always freeze them until you are ready to go carping.

Bait bands and bait floss

There are occasions when you need to mount a bait tight to the hook. One of the best ways of doing this is to use what is known as a bait band.

Bait band

These are small latex bands that are tied onto the hook or to a special fitting called a D ring that is positioned on the shank of the hook. The band is drawn through the centre of the pop-up using a baiting needle and a boile stop is inserted into the end of the band to stop it slipping back through the pop-up (see sequence below).

Bait floss

Another material that is used for tying on boilies to the hook or a D ring is bait floss. The diagram on the left shows how to tie the knot which will hold the boilie in place during the cast.

STEP-BY-STEP: USING A BAIT BAND ON A D RING RIG

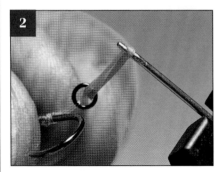

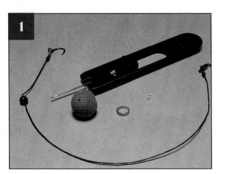

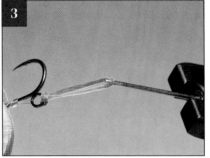

1 You will need a D rig, pop-up boile, latex band and a baiting needle.
2 Using the baiting needle pass the band through the D ring and knot it as shown.

3 Pull the knot tight and insert pop-up onto baiting needle.
4 Transfer pop-up from needle to band and hold in place using a bait stop.

Pop-ups

First of all I'd better clarify what a pop-up is, because although it will be obvious to most, there may be someone out there to whom the term is a bit unclear. For instance, one man bought a bag of pop-up mix from us and then rang up to tell us that it was no good because when he cooked his baits they didn't go POP!

A pop-up is a boilie made to float either by inserting a cork or polystyrene ball into it, using a pop-up punch, or by cooking it using a dry heat, such as microwaving, grilling or baking.

Pop-ups can be fished at varying depths up from the lake bed and are effective mainly because the carp find them easier to detect. But clever old carp may find them a bit too obvious and may therefore never fall for the trap.

Probably the easiest way to produce a pop-up boilie is to carefully bore a hole through an ordinary boilie using a boilie punch and then to insert a piece of the super-buoyant foam that comes with the punch into the core. Fox International produce good punches, available in three different sizes, namely 6mm, 8mm or 10mm and they come with different coloured strips of foam so that you can match it to the colour of your boilie.

As a guideline, the 6mm punch is for 14mm-18mm boilies, the 8mm for 20–22s and the 10mm for anything bigger than 22mm. Another simple item you can use to make a pop-up is a Gold Label Boilie Lifter. Basically these are discs of buoyant foam that you thread onto your hair rig between two halves of a boilie. The finished baits bear a little bit of a resemblance to a hamburger bun.

Yet another way of making pop-ups is to roll boilie paste around a cork or polystyrene ball and then boil them in the same way you would ordinary home-made boilies in order to make them harder, longer-lasting in the water and more resilient to the attentions of smaller fish. Again, as with a boilie punch, you will need to experiment a little to find the size of cork or polystyrene ball that will produce pop-ups of the size that you require.

Undoubtedly the best pop-ups that you can produce are made by using one of the purpose-designed pop-up mixes, as the finished baits will stay buoyant and reasonably hard for a long period of time in the water.

A number of the bait companies produce such mixes and all come with fairly easy-to-follow

▲ *Another way to make your boilie pop-up is to insert foam into the core using a boilie punch.*

instructions. Although I have no doubt that all of these mixes produce good results, the only mix I have had a lot of experience at making up is 'The Solar Perfect Pop-Up mix'.

A number of different cooking methods are described on the instructions, although my favourite method is to 'dry fry' the boilies in a non-stick frying pan. The first step is to crack an egg into a mixing bowl and then add to this the attractors, a small amount of the pop-up oil supplied and a powdered colouring if required.

Because these baits are normally only being used as hook baits, you can add more than your normal amount of attractors. This is because some of the smell will be lost as a result of the method of cooking. The next step is to mix together the egg and the attractors etc. Once this is done, add the pop-up mix until a soft paste is formed.

All that is now required is to roll out the baits by whatever means you would normally use, although you need to make them a little smaller than you intend, as the cooking method will cause them to swell a little.

Once all of your baits are rolled out it is then time to cook them. In order to do this place 20 or so baits into a non-stick frying pan, hold the pan over the full heat of a gas stove and roll the baits around, keeping the pan revolving all the time, otherwise the baits will stick to the pan and burn.

After about two minutes or so of doing this you will notice the baits start to swell slightly and turn a little lighter in colour. After a further two or three minutes the baits will start to make a sort of 'chinking' sound as they roll round the pan.

About another two minutes after this the baits should be ready. At this stage they should be tipped

STEP-BY-STEP: MAKING POP-UPS

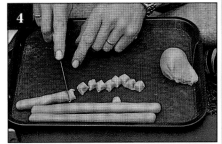

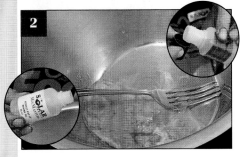

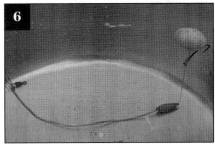

1   I'm using Solar's Perfect Pop-up mix and I'm making a three-egg mix on the bank.
2   Crack three eggs, add 25ml of the oil you get with the mix, plus 5ml of flavour.
3   Gradually add the powder base-mix and stir into the eggs until you arrive at a workable mix.

4   On a flat surface roll your mix out into a long sausage and cut in into 'chops' like this.
5   Roll by hand into balls and roll them around in a pan over the stove for about 5-7 minutes.
6   Test before use to make sure they float. Once made, they will last for ages stored in a bag.

out of the pan and onto an old cloth or tea towel in order for them to cool down completely.

So there you have it, perfect pop-ups every time, although it's worth testing one to make sure it floats.

Playing and weighing

It's time to catch that carp you've been dreaming of

Perhaps the most exciting thing about carp fishing is the bite. Those few moments when suddenly, after perhaps a long time waiting, the bite alarm suddenly shrieks and line is ripped from the Baitrunner. Your heart nearly beats out of your chest as an angry carp makes off with your hook bait at an alarming rate of knots. At this point all you really need to do is calmly pick up the rod, bend into the fish and then proceed to play it to the bank. No need for any wild striking, you're not shark fishing! The fish will already be hooked.

I'd like to think that I'm as cool as a cucumber when I get a bite, but in reality I'm a nervous wreck, because even after 30 years of carp fishing my knees still tremble and I get butterflies in my stomach. It's called 'adrenaline', and long may it continue, because this is what carp fishing is all about!

I recently read of my old mate Dave Lane's account of playing 'the big fish' on a lake that we both fish in Kent, a carp I would like to catch more than any other. In the early morning mist he'd already experienced the adrenaline rush of the bite that awoke him from his sleep, and there were a few anxious moments as he expertly played what was obviously a big carp towards the bank.

Then, in the deep, clear margins, its dark back appeared as if from nowhere. It was 'the' massive mirror carp. At this point a bit of panic set in, and he found himself in a position that he suddenly didn't want to be in. "When I saw the fish I had on the end I just wanted to throw my rod down and run away because I no longer wanted to be under that much pressure." Luckily he didn't, but that didn't restrain him from jumping into the lake

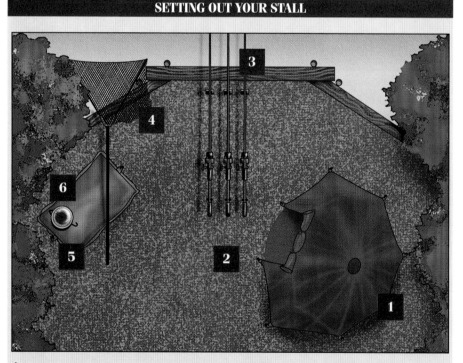

SETTING OUT YOUR STALL

1 *Position the bivvy so you can see the rods, indicators and the water out in front of you.*

2 *Note that the area behind the rods should be clear for casting.*

3 *Because this angler is fishing straight out in front of him, all three rods are pointing straight out.*

4 *The landing net is set up and is ready.*

5 *A large unhooking mat is laid out on the ground near to the net.*

6 *Scales are ready to weigh the carp.*

▲ *Lee puts the rod through its paces as he prepares to net a lively carp. Notice how the net is partly submerged so he can draw the carp into it with ease.*

with his landing net, such was his predicament. Ten minutes or so later he was grinning for the photographs and holding one of the biggest carp in the land, all 54lb of it!

Right, assuming that you've had a bite, and you've now got a carp on the end, you will need to play it carefully. Attempting to winch it straight in could end either in the hook pulling out of the carp's mouth or in your line breaking. There are two ways to yield line to compensate for a carp's powerful run. Firstly you could have your reel set with the anti-reverse in the 'off' position, so it's free to go backwards, known as 'backwinding'. Otherwise you can use the reel's clutch, whether it be on the front or on the rear of your reel. Personally I prefer the latter method, because when backwinding

you cannot always give line as quickly as it needs to be given.

At one time anglers would advocate setting the reel's clutch beforehand, but to me this is rubbish because there are so many factors that affect a clutch's performance, such as air temperature and pressure. What I generally do is to loosen the clutch off quite a bit once I've made my initial contact with the fish, and then once I am settled into the fight I tighten or loosen it accordingly.

At all times you should try to keep a tight line to the carp and you should use an easy pumping action when gaining line on it in order to bring it closer to the bank. When it's close in, you need to be particularly careful. Although it will now be tiring quite a bit, any sudden lunges it makes will be putting a lot more pressure onto your hook, line and end tackle than when it was further out, because there's less line to stretch. Try to be calm, it's nearly beaten. At this point your landing net, which should

▲ *If the rig is right most carp will be hooked in the lower lip like this.*

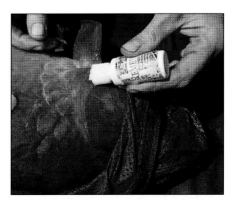

▲ *Some carp may require treatment for sores and cuts.*

have been placed in a convenient nearby position beforehand, should be placed into the marginal water in readiness.

Suddenly, the fish will be seen to tire and will start lying on its side and gulping air, letting itself to be drawn easily towards the bank. Be careful though, because they often gain a new lease of life on seeing the net, so be prepared to give it some more line. Don't stab at it with the net whatever you do, as this can spook them. Just ease it gently over the rim, and it's yours!

Now take a few moments to gain some composure before lifting the fish and net out of the water and onto the unhooking mat, because many a landing net or rod has accidentally been broken at this stage.

As for your unhooking mat, this should already have been placed in a suitable position away from the water's edge, after first having made sure it was not put on any sharp rocks or stones. If you are by yourself, it may be worth having a spare bankstick near your landing net so you can fasten your net to the bank, with the fish still in the water. Bearing in mind that at some point you may have to leave the fish unattended while you wet your weigh sling or go for your scales, be careful to secure it properly.

However, because you don't want to lose your rod, reel, landing net and the fish, if there are other people about you can get them to hold the net in the water's edge whilst you prepare to weigh your catch.

Wet your weigh sling, wring out the excess water, zero your scales with the sling hung from them and then place the scales and sling within easy reach of the unhooking mat. I would normally take this opportunity to replenish my hook bait on the other rod and recast to the same spot, because you never know, you could catch another one fairly quickly if the fish are having a feeding spell. Now lift the net with the fish inside onto the mat and then set about unhooking it. I have never needed to use forceps in order to unhook a carp, mainly because most of the time I use hooks with either crushed or very small barbs. However, it's worth having a set nearby just in case. If the fish is lively it can help to put the wet sack over its eyes to calm it down.

Once unhooked, your hook should be placed into the butt ring of your rod and the rod placed out of the way in a position where it's not likely to be trodden on. Although not absolutely essential, special fish treatment

solutions such as Solar Tackle's Remedy, Kryston's Klinik or Kevin Nash's new Medi-carp, are available should you need to treat any wounds, sores or hook marks. So please take some time to look the fish over and apply where necessary.

Now slide your carp carefully into your weigh sling in readiness for weighing. A number of different types of scales are available for weighing large fish. I use 50kg Weighmates which are expensive (over £150) but they are the business. The 60lb Reuben Heaton's are also good, but bear in mind I'm after a British record.

When weighing a heavy fish, it can be very difficult to hold it properly unless you can brace your elbows to your body. For this reason a lot of anglers are tempted to hold their scales with their hands cupped around the base, which gives a very inaccurate reading. A number of manufacturers produce longer weigh bars that clip onto the top of scales, but these are a waste of time, because you still can't brace your elbows into your body and get a proper lift on the fish.

At the Tackle Box where I work we sell a special crook called an I.S. Weight Lifter. This little gadget screws onto the female thread of a landing net pole or a long, hefty extending storm pole and is very simple to use and extremely effective for the job. To use it, simply screw it into the end of the storm pole, hook your scales onto the hook and then, with the bottom end of the pole rested against the inside of your boot, lift until the sling leaves the floor and read the scales. Whilst your fish is on the unhooking mat, it should not be left unattended at all, although if you do have to leave it for some reason, always cover it with the wet sling which should have a calming effect.

◄ *Lee says always smile when you're pictured with a big fish! So what happened Lee?*

▲ *Protect your catch and always use an unhooking mat on which to rest the carp.*

Right, it's now time to put on a big grin for the camera. I see far too many carp anglers with good fish in the press and many look miserable. You've just caught a beautiful, big fish. Be happy!

It is worthwhile to have a container full of lake water nearby when taking pictures. This can be used to douse the fish, should it be showing signs of drying out, and also to clean it up and give the skin a nice sheen. A lot of people seem to have problems holding carp for photographs, and especially so if it is a big one. Most of their problem is that they are a bit frightened of it, which is perhaps understandable, although unnecessary.

The main thing is that you need to be a bit firm with the fish and be prepared to cower your body over should it start flapping about. First, you should kneel down behind the fish and then, with one hand rested underneath it in the area of its vent and the other hand underneath it just up from its pectoral fins, slowly lift it up at the same time, bringing your elbows into your body.

If the sun is out, you should be facing the sun, and the camera should be facing away from it so you don't get any glare or shafts of light on the picture.

If you have to stand in the shade, get the photographer to use the flash for at least some of the pictures, even on a bright day. The same applies if you are wearing a cap with a brim that throws shade onto your face. Sometimes you may find it easier and more comfortable to squat down so you can rest your elbows on your knees, which will help you to support the weight of the fish.

A lot of anglers advocate putting a finger or thumb into the carp's mouth in order to calm it. Personally I'm not sure about this and have never really found that it makes very much difference. If you're holding a lively fish it will still be lively, irrespective of where your fingers and thumbs are. The wet sack over the eyes trick usually works, though. Never stand up with the fish in your arms, as one mistake like a sudden flip, and the fish could crash to the ground doing irreparable damage to itself.

With the photos done it's time to return the fish to the water. I use an unhooking mat that enables the sides to be zipped up, so it's easy to take the fish back to the water's edge contained within it. If your unhooking mat is not like this and is simply the flat, padded

type, then it's best to put the carp back into the weigh sling and take it to the water's edge in that. Whatever you use, keep the fish near the ground in case of an accident.

When you get to the water's edge be sure to pick a returning point that is safe. On a lot of waters, the swims are supported at the front by wooden stakes or scaffold poles sticking up out of the ground, so ensure that you are well clear of these. Then it's a case of removing the carp carefully from the sling or mat and lowering it gently into the water. You might have to hold the fish in the water for a few moments until it revives, although sometimes they go back in an extremely hurried state, so be prepared to get wet as your carp powers away with a flick of its tail.

Although on many waters their use is forbidden, at times you may find it necessary to use a carp sack to retain your fish for a longer period. It may be too dark to take a proper photograph or perhaps there's nobody else about to do the honours. There are a few rules that need to be followed in order to sack up a fish properly.

Firstly, use a sack that's been purposely designed and is big enough to hold the size of carp that you hope to catch. Unlike a keepnet (which shouldn't be used for large carp), you should only retain one carp per sack at any one time, otherwise the fish could damage each other. Always sack the fish up in the deepest water possible and ensure that the cord on the sack is properly secured to a bankstick firmly pushed into the ground.

You should not sack up carp in hot conditions and especially if you can't find any water deep enough to do so. Never sack up fish during droughts or when there is an algae problem, because the dissolved oxygen of the water will be extremely low. Only sack up a fish for as long as absolutely necessary to get it photographed or witnessed.

The Method

A look at Method mixes, rigs and groundbaits

The tactic known as the Method was first developed in this country in match-fishing circles, and was designed for catching carp quickly when fishing heavily-stocked carp/match waters. Having said that, those of you who are old enough to remember the tales of Mr Crabtree and his son Peter, might be interested to know that in one of the books Mr Crabtree moulded a ball of groundbait and put his hook bait in the centre of it. Was this the first ever Method rig?

The idea behind the Method is that the angler moulded a ball of groundbait around the frame of the feeder and a short hooklength was employed so that the hook was in close proximity to the pile of feed.

One of the first Method feeders to appear was the Emstat feeder which had an elastic system running through the middle. This feeder was used by match anglers where a heavy bag of fish was required in order to stand any sort of chance of winning. And devastatingly effective it was too, to the extent that the predominantly small carp would home in with gusto on the splash of the feeder,ike a shoal of piranha attacking anything resembling a live meal.

Massive bags of carp were caught as a result and the early Method users cleaned up in nearly all the matches that they entered.

Right from the very moment that the feeder settled on the lake bed their rod tip would be constantly quivering as the small carp attacked the groundbait ball. Then, with breathtaking ferocity, the tip would bend right round, almost beyond test curve proportions as another small carp succumbed to the hook bait.

This type of feeder did have its problems though, mainly because of the elastic running through its centre, which was supposed to act as a shock absorber.

They were banned on a lot of waters because a carp that broke the mainline above the feeder would often end up tethered to the rig, as it simply could not break free from the bungee-effect of the elastic.

So what exactly is the Method and why is it so effective? Well, basically it involves using a special feeder (although early Method users normally adapted their own). This has a ball of stiff groundbait formed around it and the hook bait fished on a very short link, or actually pushed into the ground bait ball.

The hook bait, which was normally a bunch of maggots, although a cold chip would probably have been equally effective, would be taken as the carp picked, nudged and fed on the groundbait.

◄ *There's a variety of ready-formulated Method mixes available for the carp angler to use, and here are some of Lee's favourites. The dry mix in the tray is in fact Vitalin dog food!*

◀ *Take your time when first choosing your swim. Look for signs like bubbling, rolling and leaping fish. Once you've made your choice, take it easy at first and don't overdo the groundbaiting. Look to get some indication from the bobbins, such as a line bite or a proper run.*

You may attract unwanted species such as bream and tench. Don't worry, the carp will soon follow. Getting anything feeding in your swim is often the key to success.

When the carp arrive, all of a sudden the bobbin will slam into the butt of the rod. Get ready for some real action Jackson!

▲ *This carp couldn't resist the mix of groundbait presented around the feeder. Note the distance from the feeder that the hook bait is positioned.*

In most cases there would be no need to strike at a bite because the carp would hook itself as it came up against the full resistance of the set-up.

Although it's a tactic that is at its most effective on venues where there is a high density of carp, it can also work extremely well for specimen carp on more sparsely stocked waters, which is what I've been targeting throughout this book.

The main reason for its effectiveness is that by having a large ball of groundbait in close proximity to your hook bait, you are drawing attention to it in much the same way as a PVA stringer or a PVA bag full of pellets

or boilies does. The one very big difference with the Method, however, is that all manner of interesting goodies can be included in the groundbait in order to make it more attractive, which is something that is not so easily done with PVA stringers or bags.

All manner of flavours, attractors, oils, live foods such as maggots, plus seeds, hemp and even pellets can be added in order to enhance the attractiveness of the mix. In fact the permutations are almost endless.

Some of the continental anglers even include things like bird droppings in their groundbait, although why carp should be attracted by this I don't know, because I should think that they are by now pretty damn sick of being pooped on from above!

With regard to tackle required for the Method it always surprises me that some of the match boys advocate the use of heavy, powerful feeder rods. Now far be it for me to criticise them for this advice, but I'd have thought that a feeder rod was far from adequate for casting a ball of groundbait weighing a good 3oz any sort of distance!

Fair enough if the waters being fished are small and all that is required is a gentle lob. However, on larger waters where sometimes greater distances need to be attained, then surely only a carp rod with a fairly hefty test curve would be suitable?

In my opinion, for what it is worth, only carp rods with a test curve of 2.75lb or above are really suitable. Don't forget that I not only use and abuse fishing tackle myself, but I also sell it for a living, therefore I have seen far too many rods that have been broken through misuse.

And it's always the same old story… "I bought this rod from your shop about a year ago, mate and was using it at the weekend and it snapped – and I was only using a half-ounce lead!" "What weights have you used in the past?" "I've used it with 2oz leads, no problem."

The end result is that the customer leaves the shop with his tail between his legs, in search of the insurance policy that he's sure that he placed in an old shoe-box tucked somewhere underneath the sink!

Take it from me, if there's a fault in the blank that a fishing rod is made from (and it does happen from time to time) then the rod will normally break during the first few times that it is put into use.

If the rod breaks a year later then this is usually down to misuse and there is no better

way of misusing a rod that is not suitable than by fishing the Method!

The only other important item of tackle to consider if you choose to use the Method is your mainline. You must bear in mind the weight of the ball of groundbait that you mould around your feeder, in addition to the weight of the feeder itself.

Unless you are casting it for only a short distance, you should be using a mainline with a breaking strain of at least 12lb, although I think that 15lb would be an even better choice. For fishing at extreme distance, however, it may be necessary to drop down in line diameter, therefore reducing the breaking strain, in order to attain a greater distance. A shock leader of roughly 20ft

of 25lb breaking strain line will be needed to take the initial brunt of the cast.

Apart from that, all the rest of your tackle should be more than adequate.

Now for the feeder itself. Although there are various different types of Method feeder available, my own preference is for the Richworth In-line feeders. These are available in two different weights, either 1oz or 2oz. The size to choose is obviously down to the distance that you intend fishing. If you choose the heavier version then your rod and mainline must be up to the job.

The Richworth In-line feeder was invented by John Hofgartner and there are some pictures here of the early prototype models John played around with before the development of the in-line feeder most of us now use.

These feeders are used in much the same way that you would use an in-line lead and are threaded onto your mainline and in turn rest up against your hooklink swivel.

Used in this way, they are free to slide up your mainline, although if you wish to use them semi-fixed, as I do most of the time, then they are fairly easy to adapt. In order to do this, all that you do is simply to superglue a short length of 2mm diameter silicone

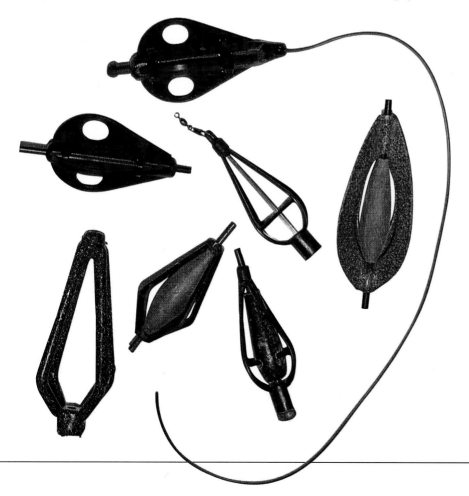

◀ This picture shows a variety of prototype Method feeders that Richworth-backed carp angler John Hofgartner put together before inventing the finished feeder, which is at the top. This style of feeder is regarded as the best, and is widely used by carp anglers. The fin structure allows a good amount of feed to be moulded around the frame of the feeder. The finished product can be fished in-line and semi-fixed, too, so it is very fish-friendly.

rubber onto the section of plastic tube that protrudes from the bottom of the feeder. Then your hooklink swivel pulls into the silicone in order to semi-fix it in place.

The main reason for doing this is because when a fish is feeding on your groundbait, if and when it takes your hook bait, it comes up against the weight of your feeder and whatever groundbait is left moulded around it, which will lead to a self-hooking situation, hopefully at least!

There are other ways of fitting this feeder and if you look at the picture sequences you will be able to pick a set-up to suit your own style of fishing.

All I would add to this is that the feeder must be set up with safety in mind. If the carp breaks the mainline the feeder must be able to drop free from the line. Fixed rigs and heavy shockleaders will not allow the carp to rid itself of the feeder and could end up leading to a tethered fish.

Another recent innovation, and again one produced by Richworth, is the Paste Feeder Bomb. Although these were initially designed to have paste moulded around, they are also perfect for using the Method.

The good thing about these Paste Bombs is that because they are like a conventional lead weight, apart from their shape, it's very quick and easy to adapt a conventional carp set-up to one that is suitable for using the Method. Again, like the In-Line feeders, the Paste Bombs are available in a number of different sizes, ranging from 1.5oz up to around 3.5oz.

There are a number of ways that a Paste Bomb can be set up. However, I prefer to use them on a relatively simple set-up which I

'What you should really be doing is trying to build up the swim and therefore attracting more and more fish to it.'

use for most of my carp fishing.

This involves a length of anti-tangle tubing pushed into a tail rubber which is then pushed on to the back of a Kevin Nash Safety Bolt Rig clip.

Once the bomb is in place my hooklink swivel then pulls into the front of the clip and then, of course, the hooklink hangs down from this. Most of the time when using the Method, and whether using a feeder or a Paste Bomb, I prefer to use an extremely short hooklink of around three to four inches. This allows the hook bait to be fished in close proximity to the ground bait around the feeder.

Some anglers prefer to present their hook bait actually moulded in with the groundbait around the feeder, but I sometimes worry that it may end up buried on the underside of the feeder once it has settled on the lake bed.

It probably doesn't matter a great deal even if it is underneath the feeder though, because the groundbait ball probably gets rolled around quite a bit once the carp are feeding on it. Therefore the bait should be

◄ *The paste bomb is semi-fixed in place with the aid of a Nash safety clip and a tail rubber. If the lead should get trapped it can be broken free from the clip with ease simply by applying pressure with the rod.*

dislodged from the groundbait and into a position where the carp can pick it up and get hooked.

Even so, I'll stick with having my hook bait a short distance from the feeder and not moulded into the mix. This is mainly because that is what I've had the most success with in my own experience.

One thing that is important when using the Method is to make sure you replenish the groundbait around the feeder fairly regularly. Although there will still be quite a lot of attraction in the vicinity of your hook bait, if you leave it out for a long period of time the carp will not be looking for more food and they will move away to someone else's swim, which can be frustrating.

What you should really be doing is trying to build up the swim and therefore attracting more and more fish to it, hopefully getting them grubbing around in search of food. This is Method fishing at its very best.

What I generally do when I make up my groundbait by the waterside is to drop a ball of it (roughly the same size as what I'm moulding around the feeder) into the margins. Then I time how long it takes for the groundbait to break down. By doing this I get a fairly good indication of when it's necessary to have a recast.

It's strange really, because Method fishing seems to go against the grain of normal specimen carp fishing. Normally, if you were to cast an ordinary carp set-up with boilies or whatever in the vicinity of a carp they would get really spooked, and often never come back!

With the Method, however, it seems that the carp are a lot more tolerant. They cannot resist swimming up close to investigate a great big ball of food. What all this means is that you can often get away with murder!

STEP-BY-STEP: JACKSON'S METHOD MIX

1 Lee uses Van Den Eynde mixes for the Method, which are mixed 50–50.
2 A 1oz feeder is used and is fitted to the line in an in-line fashion.
3 The hooklength is semi-fixed to the feeder.
4 Water is added to the groundbait. When the mix is stiff, mould it around the frame.
5 The feeder is now completely encased in the mix and the hook bait is left to hang free.
6 Shape the bottom end of the mix like a rocket nose, so the feeder is easy to cast.

Now, there are no hard or fast rules as to the amount of free offerings to use when fishing the Method, but I generally fire in about four golf-ball-sized balls of groundbait in the vicinity of my hook bait and Method feeder after every cast.

One thing that is very important is to memorise the spot that you have cast to and then keep everything plugging away around this same area. If your groundbait is spread out too far, then you stand a good chance of the carp eating too much – the fish could

then go off the feed without you ever getting a chance of nailing it.

Obviously the better you have chosen your spot in the first place, the more successful you will be. But sometimes with the Method, a duff spot can be turned into a productive one quite quickly!

Day session

How to tackle a day ticket water in less than favourable conditions

The particular day's fishing shown in this chapter was in mid-February, but it will not be unlike many of the days you experience through much of the winter and spring. Even right up until May the weather will still be cold and biting winds very much with us. For me the old close season is still very much fishing from winter into spring.

Indeed, in the great Dick Walker's time, it was thought that carp were impossible to catch in the winter and that they spent their time buried deep in the mud until spring, when the days once more become longer and warmer. Obviously Dick and his friends were mistaken, otherwise we would never see any carp captures appearing in the angling press during this period, which of course we undoubtedly do.

I do sometimes wonder though if in a lot of instances these anglers of old were right. Because although carp are regularly caught at this time of year, on many waters they appear to 'switch off' with the coming of the first frosts and then nothing is seen, let alone caught, until about March.

For this reason the correct choice of water is paramount if you are to stand any sort of chance of latching on to a cold water carp, so you should always consider yourself lucky if and when you do.

So what do I deem to be a water where you will stand a higher than average chance of catching a cool pool carp?

Contrary to what you might think or believe, I think that shallower waters with average water depths of six feet or less offer the best chance. Shallow waters are warmed much quicker in the event of a sunny winter's day, and they are generally better oxygenated by the effects of wind.

Both of these factors are more likely to stir a carp into life, in which case, if it starts to have a little swim about it will be using up energy. This means that it will need to have a little feed in order to replenish lost energy.

On deeper waters, however, because the hours of light are relatively short during the winter, no matter how warm the sun might be it's never out for long enough to make any sort of difference to the water temperature and wake the carp from their torpid state.

Carp stock is another thing to take into consideration. The best winter waters to fish are those that are heavily stocked with carp, as these will offer you the best chance of

some fishing action. Waters with sparse stocks of carp will be difficult, even in the height of summer. Therefore to consider this type of water in the wintertime with the hope of catching a carp is bordering on madness!

Angler pressure is another consideration. If the water is fairly heavily fished then more free bait will be going in. In addition, there is more chance of the fish being disturbed by the constant actions of casting and leads thumping about the lakebed.

So why am I writing about winter carp fishing in this chapter?

Well, winter makes up a good half of the year in this country, and is a time when it will probably be more difficult to make a catch. So, if you are considering a bit of winter carp fishing, the information on these pages should be of some help.

My choice of water for this session was Capstone Country Park, near Gillingham, in Kent. It is a small water which is well stocked with carp, has average depths of less than six feet throughout and, because it can be fished on a day ticket, it is fairly heavily fished – perfect I think!

Oh no! Is that the alarm clock already... I've only just gone to sleep!

5:45 As soon as I put the windscreen wipers on the windscreen froze.

◀ *Start the day on the right track with a steaming hot cup of tea!*

▲ *When fishing short sessions Lee sets his rods up at home. This means he can get a baited hook out before the sun rises.*

Perhaps I should go roach fishing instead, it doesn't look all that good a day for carp. Still, at least it's dry and you never know it could turn out to be 80 degrees today – 40 this morning and 40 this afternoon! The wind is chilly, too, which would indicate to me that it has got a bit of an easterly direction to it.

6.00 Brrrrr! We're going to need all the thermals on today, boys and girls! This Pertex clothing really is the business and, with my thermal boots as well, I'm not going to get cold.

Although you are not permitted to start fishing until 7 a.m. on this water, I always like to arrive early at any venue so that I can take my time and have a little look around in order to assess the day ahead.

Also, because it's a popular water, you need to arrive early if you want to get a better choice of swim. Once the day is in full swing, it's not always possible to move if you see a bit of carp activity elsewhere. Chances are there will be another angler already occupying that swim. Initial swim choice in this situation is vital – pick the wrong one and you'll have to wait until next time. Pick the right one then all is well and good.

In an ideal world I would like to have walked around the lake yesterday and the day before. Time spent walking around watching the water prior to fishing and talking to the anglers who are fishing is often a short cut to sorting out where to fish on the day you turn up.

Remember, though, one good turn always deserves another, so if someone turns up

▶ *After having his rod licence checked, Lee buys his day ticket.*

and asks me how things are going on the day that I'm fishing, I always try to give them as much information and help as I possibly can. That said, I cannot abide green-eyed monsters, so if I've had a bit of a result and I hear that a person I have told is stabbing me in the back, then they don't get helped again! I think today is going to be a bit of a struggle, unfortunately.

There is a fairly brisk northeasterly wind blowing that is keeping the air and water

▲ *As the lead lands, the rod is placed on the floor and the loosefeed is fired out to where the lead has landed.*

▲ *The rod is then placed on the rest...*

▲ *... and the bobbin is then placed on the line.*

temperatures chilled. In such conditions it is often best to fish with the wind blowing on to your back, because water temperatures can be a degree or so warmer in the sheltered area of a lake. This can make all the difference in cold water conditions. It is also more comfortable to fish in this position. No such luck today though, as there are already a few other anglers over there.

My second choice would perhaps be a nice, close-in, snaggy area with overhanging branches or bushes. Being a tidy little park lake, though, there aren't really any such areas here offering a snaggy swim. There is one area where a bush overhangs a bit, but I seem to recall that when I had a little stroll round the lake back in the summer, the water

underneath was only a foot or so deep – a bit too shallow to find a winter carp.

6.50 It's getting quite light now, so I'm able to see most of the lake. Now, if the lake's surface was calm, I'd be looking for any little sign to give me a clue as to where to fish. Even a single bubble seen breaking on the surface can be worth an investigation, if that is all to be seen. No chance today though: the surface is quite ruffled, so it is very unlikely that anything much will be on show.

It's at times like this that the only real option is to call on past experience. If you have fished the water a number of times before in the winter and have caught or have seen a carp or two caught, these are the areas to choose. Winter carp get very 'hot spotted' and are likely to be found and caught in the same area again and again. Even if you haven't fished the water for a year or two, winter carp rarely change their habits. So, what was a hot spot last year will still probably still be one for a number of years to follow, so at least this will be a fairly good starting point. My swim choice for today is going to be down towards the far end of the lake at its widest point. Although the lake is relatively small, I always favour the middle, if in doubt.

There are still 15 minutes or so before the day ticket office opens, so I think I'll make a quick brew of tea to warm the old cockles. Christine, my faithful old stove, can be a bit temperamental and has a habit of flaring up on the first burn of the day. However, on cold mornings like this a steaming hot, fresh cup of tea or coffee on the bank is most welcome.

7.00 The ticket office is open now so I've popped round there, bought my ticket from the machine and then popped into the office to announce my swim number. At this particular water I show the man my rod licence as requested. I must admit, I find it quite reassuring to have my licence checked. If licences were checked more on waters throughout the country then fewer people would get away with dodging. The Environment Agency would gain more revenue and our waters might perhaps benefit as a result. That said, in my opinion licences should be done away with altogether and instead a 30p or so increase should be put on everyone's water rates in order to pay for the upkeep of our rivers, canals and stillwaters. At the end of the day it is to everyone's advantage that these are kept in a clean and tidy condition.

Back to swim 12. I always carry my rods already rigged-up and ready to go, which is a big advantage in the winter because it saves the discomfort of setting them up with cold hands.

All I need to do is unclip them from my tackle sling, push the sections together, at the same time lining up the eyes, put some

▲ *This is the amount of free offerings used. On the first cast of the day Lee feeds about 9-10 free offerings around each hook bait.*

STEP-BY-STEP: GETTING THE BEST FROM BOILIES IN COLD WATER

1 A broken boilie is a better bait in the cold as it is able to leak out the flavour quickly.

2 The two halves are presented on a hair, and a small boilie stop holds them in place.

3 A long mono hooklength is the order of the day in a bid to get a run.

baits onto the rig and then cast them out – easy! By the time the angler up the bank has rigged-up his two rods from scratch, I've already had two more cups of tea and a couple of biscuits!

My rigs for today are fairly simple (as they normally are). Semi-fixed 2oz Korda distance leads attached to Kevin Nash Safety Bolt Rig clips and an 18-inch length of 0.75mm anti-tangle tubing attached above the clip by the way of a coned-shaped piece of rubber known as a Tail Rubber. I use 16-inch hooklinks using 8lb Gold Label Pro Gold monofilament. A size 8 Kamasan B175 hook, with the hair rig formed by tying the knotless knot, completes the rig.

The bait that I've chosen for today is one of my all-time winter favourites, Richworth 14mm frozen Tutti-Frutti boilies. For my hook baits, rather than using them conventionally, I have cut a boilie in half and then mounted the two halves onto the hair. By doing this I'm presenting the carp with a shape that they are not used to seeing or, more to the point, 'feeling' in their mouths. Plus, by cutting the boilie in half it will more readily leak the flavour off into the surrounding area. As I said earlier, conditions are not ideal, so I don't think that there is a need for free offerings as

▶ *Talking to other anglers on the water will give you an idea of what's been caught or if any area of the lake has been producing better than others.*

I don't really think that the carp are going to be wanting to eat an awful lot today.

That said, I do like to have a few 'freebies' in the vicinity of my hook bait in order to attract attention to it. Also, I haven't seen any of the other nine or so anglers put any in, or rather I have, but the seagulls swooped down and got all of them. So I think I'll put a few out in order to be a bit different from the rest. In these situations I would normally attach a PVA 'stringer' of free offerings to my hook before casting. However, as this lake is fairly small I should easily be able to catapult a cluster of freebies accurately around each hook bait.

What I do is this. First I fill the catapult pouch with as many boilies as it will take – in this case, about ten 14mm baits with my pouch. Then I position the catapult very near

to the place that I'm going to cast from. I then make the cast and as soon as the lead hits the surface I place the rod on the ground and pick up the catapult. Next I catapult the bait out as accurately as I can to the circle left from where the lead has landed. Plop! That's two for the seagulls and eight for the carp – that'll do!

I've got to admit that today the wind is making aiming a little difficult, so I wasn't as accurate as I would have liked when placing the bait. I'm not really happy with how the cast went, and the freebies didn't land 'spot on'. Never mind, Jacko, put it down to a lack of practice and accept that it's going to be a bad day – better luck next time, mate! About all that is now left to do is to have some more tea, scan the water for a sign or two and then sit back and wait.

◄ *Not a big fish but it doesn't matter. Nobody else on the lake has caught.*

Nothing wrong with that! Perhaps the swirls we'd both seen had been caused by pike, because neither of us had actually seen the fish that caused the swirl. I'm fairly certain that if they had been carp then he would have received some sort of action, even if it was only a line bite caused by one of them swimming into his lines.

9.00 All is very quiet on the bobbin front. As far as I know, of the ten anglers fishing here today, including myself, nobody has had any sort of action at all. I'm not that surprised by this, because even if the conditions had been better, on most waters in winter I generally find the most productive periods fall somewhere between 11 a.m. and 3 p.m., so the best is hopefully still to come.

I've decided to fish one rod statically and to leave it in position with a few free offerings around it. The other rod I'm recasting fairly regularly, each time to a slightly different spot. By doing this you can sometimes land near to some carp which, although not feeding, might just move in to investigate the disturbance caused.

Of course this could equally have an adverse effect and spook them. Generally though, in winter I find the carp to be a bit more tolerant of disturbance. It's probably because they are in a state of semi-sleep most of the time !

The trouble with this water is that it's small and so there are only so many different spots that can be covered without interfering with other angler's lines. So all that I can hope for is that if there are any fish out in

► *The waiting game is getting longer and time is running out!*

front of me, they will suddenly wake up and have a little feed.

10.30 In the last half hour I have seen a couple of fish (or it could have been the same one twice) show themselves close in, in front of the angler in the first swim, which is about 60 yards down to my left. I wouldn't really have expected them to be there, because the cold wind is blowing straight into him.

I think I'll wander down for a bit of a chat. Sure enough, he'd seen them too and had positioned his hook baits in the area where the swirling fish showed. We had a little chat about this and that and what bait he was using. Nashy's Whisky boilies!

11.45 A buzzer sounds on the opposite side of the lake from me, and an angler leaps into action. His mate is by his side with the landing net at the ready, but suddenly they both walk off in disgust! He's lost it! I don't like seeing people lose fish and especially on a day like today where any carp caught would be a bonus. I've been on the receiving end a few times myself in the past, and the feeling left inside you is not very nice, especially if the carp that is lost looks or feels like a big one.

It does happen from time to time though, and sometimes even to the most experienced angler. In situations like this I always try to console myself with the fact that if I've done nothing wrong, and my tackle hasn't let me

◄ The broken boilie bait has done the trick.

2.00 Well, if they did come onto the feed it must have been only for about five minutes because, apart from the fish that was lost, nothing else has happened anywhere on the lake. There's no point in putting any more free offerings in – there is already enough out there and any more might worsen the situation, if that's possible!

3.00 It's getting a bit frustrating now. Although the conditions are unfavourable, I would have thought that something would have happened by now. My eyelids are now starting to get a little heavy, probably due to the effects of the wind and the fairly early start that I made.

Perhaps the carp are sitting at mid-water, which they sometimes do in winter. I'll reel in a rod and put on a pop-up hook bait to fish mid-water. This is a method that I've occasionally had some success with in the past when all else has failed. The area I'm fishing is roughly six feet deep so I'll put on a three-foot hooklength and fish the pop-up straight up off the lead.

Sometimes when fishing like this, casting can be a little difficult, especially if you're using a hooklength of six feet long or more. This is because your bait snags the ground and the undergrowth while you are trying to cast. What I generally do in this case is to place a cup down on the ground behind my casting position and then place my hook bait inside it prior to casting. Although casting will be a little more awkward than normal, at least you know that your bait is in the clear.

4.30 Not long to go now. They'll be closing the park gates in half an hour or so. I've reeled in the long link with the pop-up on now. I've given it a little trial, but all to no avail. The problem with fishing like this is that you can never be sure at what level the carp could be, between the lakebed and the surface.

I'm sure that if you could get it right on the day then some real bumper catches could be made. This is where us carp anglers fall a long way short of our match-fishing cousins. They thoroughly explore the depths with their end tackle, although the difference is that they are generally trying to catch those fish that are present in far greater numbers than we specimen carp anglers.

4.45 I think I'll have a slow packup now: everything apart from the rods and landing net, that is. Beep! About time, that was cutting it fine! This may seem a bit of a false, made-up-ending, I can assure you that it is not. At least there's one carp in this lake that wants to be famous and get its picture in print.

I'm taking it ever so easy playing this one because I really don't want to lose it. Also, I'm having to take it a little bit easy because I'm using a braided mainline. Because of its total lack of stretch you have to be more than a little careful in case the hook pulls out or the hooklink breaks. Gently does it Jacko! Wait for the fish to wallow over on its side and then draw it over the landing net. Yesss!

The carp looks below average size for this water and the scales confirm this. Nevertheless, at 11lb it is very welcome and has managed to put a smile back on my face. I'm going to slip it back, re-bait my rod, and then cast it out to the same spot, as there's still 15 minutes left before the gates close, so you never know! No such luck today though.

So there you have it, a day's winter carp fishing. On a normal winter's day on this water with more favourable weather conditions, I would've expected to perhaps have caught three or four carp, but this is how it goes, sometimes.

down in some way, then it's just one of those things and I wasn't meant to land it. Nevertheless, the feeling is still sickening and can last a long time, especially if you're fishing a water that contains some of the biggest carp in the country! One small consolation is that they might be coming on to the feed, so I'll position my chair a little closer to the rods.

The other angler's hook baits are not a long way from mine, despite the fact that we are fishing opposite each other. If a small group of carp have come onto the feed then I want to be ready for them. I always imagine winter carp to be tightly bunched together in little, or perhaps sometimes big, groups. If one of the group of fish decides to feed, then I would think that most of the others will be likely to follow suit.

We can only guess sometimes at what is going on below the water surface, but this is how I perceive winter carp's behaviour to be.

Night fishing

How to set about fishing in the dark

The wind is rustling the leaves, an owl hoots in the not too far off distance and lightning flashes on the horizon as the last train of the night speeds by. A screeching from the bushes signifies some unsuspecting animal being murdered, a bat swoops through the air and sets the bite alarm falsely bleeping as it brushes the line. The coots cry out as a monstrous fish crashes out in the darkness... Yes, you've guessed it, I'm night fishing! I hope I don't get a bite and I wish that this sleeping bag was longer, so that I could get my head a little further into it!

This is how I felt when I was only 16 years old, and at that age the idea of night fishing really appealed to me, until it got dark anyway! I'm not at all sure when my frame of mind changed, but now I'm intrigued by the noises and occurrences of the night, instead of being scared to death by them. Sure I've had some scary moments, such as fairly

close encounters with a wild boar, a very abrupt awakening when a Great Dane dog sniffed my nose at 2 a.m. and having a mole make its way to ground level inside my bivvy. I've had rats in my rucksack, a slug sealing my eyelids shut with its slime, and even an Elvis impersonator blue-suede-shoeing his way past my swim in the early hours, on every occasion that I night fished on one particular water!

Well, I'm now quite a bit older than 16 and, despite doing thousands of nights ever since, the bogey man hasn't got me yet! You come to realise that the only difference between night and day time fishing is that it's dark, so you can't see as well. And the only reason you notice more noises is because sound travels more in darkness. Also many wild animals hunt at night so that they are less detectable.

In order to be efficient at night fishing you need to be well organised and things need to

be strategically placed, so that you know where to find them. Obviously the most important item to be placed where you can find it is your torch, because without this you are lost. I can remember being approached by a nearby angler asking to borrow my torch so that he could find his! I did have a little snigger to myself.

Some anglers choose to have a Tilley type lamp lighting up their swim and all the surrounding area. Perhaps I'm a little old fashioned, but to me the idea of night fishing is to blend in with the darkness, so I would never dream of using such a thing – and I find it annoying when other people do. Fair enough to have a fairly dim light within the confines of your bivvy, but if I wanted to admire the bright lights then I'd do a night or two on Blackpool beach!

The thing is, if you cut down on using a light as much as possible then you gain a fair degree of night vision and it's surprising how much you can see. I find head torches to be far better than any other light, purely and simply because they leave you with both hands completely free. With conventional torches you need to hold them in your mouth if you need to undertake a task using two hands, with the result that you normally end up dribbling all over the place.

There are a number of different head torches now available, but I favour those

◀ *In the cover of darkness the biggest carp feed without fear.*

made by the company Petzl, and in particular the Petzl Zoom head torch. Petzl are the main type of head torches used by potholers and by the emergency services, so if they're good enough for a sometimes life or death situation, then they should be more than reliable enough for fishing. I got my head torch from Leeda Tackle.

If you require any type of lighting inside your bivvy, then by far the best that I have come across is the Bushlite candle lantern from Gardner Tackle. One trouble that you may experience with battery-type lighting is that the batteries never seem to last for very long, which can prove a costly exercise. Bushlite candle burners, however, use relativel cheap-to-buy conventional household candles. Each candle burns for a long time, somewhere between four and five hours which should be more than sufficient for most night fishing trips.

▲ *As the sun slips away Lee's baits are already in position, leaving him free to settle down, open a good book and dream of catching the biggest carp in the lake.*

Apart from a torch, the only other extra items that are required for a night session are a sleeping bag and extension cables and box for your bite alarms if you are a heavy sleeper.

I can imagine some people reading this thinking – 'sleeping bag? Why do you need this when you are supposed to be awake all night fishing?'

Well, I'm sorry to disappoint you, but most of my own night fishing is carried out before packing up in order to set off for work the following morning. Therefore, if I had stayed awake all night then I wouldn't be in much of a fit state to work would I?

Occasionally I do like to sit awake in order to look and listen for signs of carp. By and large, though, my baits are set in position before dark and then life is resumed in much the same way as if I was indoors. In other words, I go to sleep when I get tired and hope that my sleep is abruptly broken by a screaming alarm and an angry carp making off with my bait – and it does occasionally happen, despite what many people think!

Of course, if you are able to stay awake all night then you stand a slightly better chance of catching a night-time carp. But remember that at some time you will get tired, therefore the day anglers will be far more alert and vigilant whilst you are dozing!

It's all very well thinking that you can do without sleep, but unless you are on some form of drug then you can't. You need to weigh up when the

best chance of catching a carp is. Personally I find that most waters are far more productive during the day, therefore this is the time that I want to be at my best, in which case I welcome a good night's sleep.

If, on the other hand, night time is found to be best, then you need to get as much sleep as you can during the day, so that you can stay awake as long as possible during the night. The problem with this is that it can play havoc with your body clock, and it may be a long time before your body resumes normal functioning. It's a bit like jet lag or doing shift work. We were born to be awake during the day and to sleep at night, so anything that interferes with this normal procedure is bound to affect our body or mind in some way or other.

I mentioned sleeping bags, and sometimes there can be a lot of confusion as to what to buy. Sleeping bags are normally season rated, so this should be self-explanatory, but unfortunately it's not. A three-season rated sleeping bag should, as the description suggests, be good enough for the autumn.

▼ It's 3 a.m. and all Lee's planning and preparation has paid off!

However, if you get a cold night in September or October then you will probably get cold in it. As a rough guideline, I would suggest a three season sleeping bag for spring and summer use and a four or five season rated bag for autumn and winter use.

Another thing with sleeping bags is that man-made fillings, such as Hollofil or Quallofil, are much more suited for fishing use than natural fillings, such as feather and down. The reason for this is that man-made fillings will still retain their thermal qualities even when the sleeping bag is wet or damp.

One final point before moving on. A lot of anglers make the mistake of climbing into their sleeping bags with too many clothes on. Sleeping bag fillings work because your body heat warms the tiny hollows within the fibres, so by wearing too many clothes, especially if they are waterproof clothes, you will stop the filling from being able to do its job and you may well get cold.

Some form of shelter will be required in order to protect you from the elements when night fishing. Most of my own night fishing trips are short overnight sessions before setting off to work in the morning. Therefore, a 60-inch brolly with

sewn-on mini storm sides such as the Kevin Nash Profile umbrella is perfect for the job. Another good thing about this umbrella is that it affords you a good view of the water whilst still offering ample protection, so for me it's perfect.

For longer sessions and for winter use it's nice to have a fully enclosed bivvy system. This offers more space for storing away and protecting extra tackle items, as well as being that little bit warmer and cosier.

There are even a few anglers who take along a portable TV in order to pass away the hours whilst waiting for a bite. I can well imagine some people frowning on this but to me, provided they are not bothering anybody else by having the volume up too loud, this is fine. Fishing is about enjoying yourself. Once the baits are out in position it's very much a waiting game, so if some people want to occupy this time by watching *Eastenders* then so be it!

Personally I like to sit out and watch the water as much as possible because I might just see or hear that extra little sign that tells me where the fish are. Sometimes though, and especially if the conditions are a bit ugly, I like to sit back and relax and get my head stuck into a book or magazine – normally on the subject of fishing, of course.

Now bivvies take on a number of different forms. Some are normal umbrellas with what is known as an overwrap thrown over the top. Some are sort of umbrellas with storm sides permanently attached, such as the Nash Titan or the Fox Evolution Bivvy. And some bear more of a resemblance to a proper tent and are twin skinned and have a sewn-in groundsheet. Whatever you choose, I'd suggest buying something that has got a good track record for both performance and reliability. If that choice comes down to a dome-type tent then ensure that it is possible to buy spares in the event of a pole breaking.

Unfortunately, in this country the weather can be a bit unpredictable. It may be nice and calm when you leave home or at the start of your session, but it can cut up rough at times, and very quickly too, and this is when things get damaged. Occasionally a shelter will get damaged due to faulty workmanship, but in most instances it is due to improper use or an act of God when conditions really do get wild! About all you can hope for in this instance is that the shop keeper or manufacturer shows a little sympathy and helps you out with the repairs.

Well, now to the fishing itself. The only difference between fishing at night and fishing during the day is that it's dark at night, so you cannot see quite so well. As I mentioned earlier, the key to efficient night fishing is to have everything organised and in a position where you can easily find it.

Your unhooking mat should be placed in a safe position away from the water's edge

with your weigh sling strategically placed beside it. Your weighing scales need to be kept as dry as possible, and so should be kept inside your bivvy in a position where you can find them easily. Your landing net needs to be placed where it can be reached easily, bearing in mind that you may be fishing with one or more rods. On the bottom section of the handle of my own landing net I've got a two-foot length of bright yellow beachcaster butt shrink tube. This may not look very 'carpy' but it ensures that I can easily find it and, more importantly, that I don't tread on it. It's also worth having a few spare rigs tied up in case of a snap off or tangle.

Electronic bite alarms are obviously a big advantage when night fishing, and bobbins fitted with some form of night light will help give you a visual indication of what is occurring. Most modern-day bobbins have the facility to fit a night light. Starlights last up to about ten hours. For longer-term use you can fit your bobbins out with betalights which, although a lot more expensive, do glow for anything up to about ten years, so they can work out cheaper in

▲ *Dawn is often a good time to spot carp swirling on the surface. A bait cast to a moving fish can often result in its capture.*

the long term. What you choose really depends on how often you intend to night fish or fish on into the darkness.

Make sure that you buy the correct size to fit in your bobbins because they come in a number of different sizes. If in doubt you should take your bobbins along to the shop with you in order to check that they fit.

Another thing to consider is what you are going to eat and drink during your night trip, especially if your session is going to extend for more than just the night. Thermos flasks do not keep drinks hot for ever, plus I find that tea or coffee tastes fairly disgusting after only a short period when kept in one. It's far better to equip yourself with a small stove so that you can make yourself a fresh brew or maybe, if you're feeling very adventurous, a full-blown dinner.

To me, the cooking side of it is all is part of the enjoyment because it gives you something to do, and food always seems to taste that little bit better when prepared outdoors.

which means you will stand a chance of another bite or two.

Recasting to the same position further out into the lake is a lot more difficult, especially if the lake's surface is ruffled by wind. What I generally do while it's still light is line everything up with marks on the far horizon – it might be a building or a tall tree. This will give you a good indication of where to recast, and all that you need to do is to judge the distance.

What I sometimes do if I think that the spot where I have cast is a banker is, once I've cast out, to tighten up to my lead still in a standing position and then mark my line just above my reel with Tippex. I normally paint on a fairly long length of about three inches or so, so that it can be seen easily if it comes to recasting. If I then get a bite and need to recast to approximately the same spot (I say approximately because you can never cast to exactly the same spot again), once the fish has been dealt with and I've given myself some time to regain some night vision, I cast to the mark on the horizon but a bit further out. Then I reel back until the Tippex mark is just above the reel once more.

I don't leave it at that though, because I might have picked up some weed or other debris on my hook point when pulling back, which will impede the hook from penetrating if another carp picks up my bait. What I then do is to pull off a couple of yards of line from my reel and clip my line behind the line clip on the reel's spool. It's then a case of recasting, in which case the clip should brake the cast and the hook bait should land in roughly the same area. Practice makes perfect when doing this and it is something

I take along a great big wok, and after many years of practice am able to prepare some fairly exquisite dishes on the bank. In fact, my swim often gets populated with other anglers when the smell of cooking starts to waft about. Funny that! I have to smile sometimes, because when I enquire if anyone else would like some food, plates, dishes and cutlery quite conveniently appear from pockets and inside coats! I guess that it is fairly normal to carry things like this about on a stroll round the lake!

As far as stoves are concerned, there are many different versions available. Most run on gas cylinders of some type, although my favourite are the Coleman stoves that run on unleaded petrol.

A little tip though. If you buy a Coleman stove then for more efficient operation they are best run on premium unleaded petrol as opposed to the super unleaded plus. I always add some Redex petrol treatment to the fuel, as this helps to keep the workings of the stove clean and free from carbon deposits. Beware though, petrol is obviously very volatile, so if you need to refill your stove with fuel then do so well away from your bivvy and out of the way of any naked flames such as cigarettes and candle lanterns etc. An acquaintance of mine had a little accident which led to his bivvy burning down! He was lucky because he escaped unscathed and his tackle was insured – you may not be as lucky, so be careful.

The positioning of your hook baits, in other words where you cast, is obviously a lot more difficult during a night trip because you cannot see so well. As I said before though, if you keep the use of lights down to a minimum then you will be able to see a whole lot better. In an ideal world you should get your hook baits all set and in position before it gets dark. This way at least they will be in the position that you think that they should be to start with.

One thing to bear in mind is that at night carp often come in a fair bit closer to the bank, mainly because there is less disturbance. Therefore it's worth positioning at least one of your baits in a close-in spot. The closer the better, and if you do get a bite during the night then you should easily be able to reposition your bait in the same spot, that can be practised in daylight in order to get used to what you are doing.

A couple of things to remember: first, don't forget to take the line out of the clip before setting your rod in the rod rests, otherwise it might get pulled in. Second, always scrape off the Tippex mark between your fingernails at the end of your session, unless you are certain that when you return you are going to fish the same swim.

Playing a fish in darkness can sometimes be a little tricky. Try as much as possible to keep your rod tip up fairly high, which makes it easier to ascertain the fish's position. You should have checked out the whereabouts of any nearby snags, such as overhanging trees or bushes, whilst it was still daylight, so you should know when you need to put on some extra pressure.

Unlike in daylight, I don't normally dip my landing net and draw the fish over it. Instead I prefer to keep it by my side on the bank, and then, once the fish is seen to be wallowing on its side and beaten, I hastily dip the net under the fish and quickly scoop it up.

Now is the time to try to remain calm and take a moment to gain some composure. Where have you positioned your unhooking

mat? How are you going to lift the net and fish from the water as well as your rod? Where are your torch, forceps, scales and anything else that you're likely to need?

Plan it all out in your head, the fish is OK, as it's still in the landing net, in the water and there's no rush. If you intend to sack the fish until morning (if this is allowed), do so where the margins are deep and make sure that the sack cord is securely attached to a bankstick that has been pushed firmly into the ground. Ideally, you should have checked out the margins before darkness fell.

Time to re-bait and recast. Check out your rig and make sure it's not damaged. Check out your hook point to make sure it has not turned over. If in doubt, tie on a new

rig, because if the one that you're about to cast out is damaged in any way then it will fail you should you get another bite. Turn all the lights off and give yourself some time to get back some night-vision before recasting.

Sploosh! That's it, it landed about right. Beep beep – the bite alarm is set. A few more freebies, maybe? No, there's probably plenty of free bait still out there, so you don't want to further disturb or spoil your swim.

Check out the sack to make sure it's lying properly and that the fish is nice and calm inside. Wow! You can see the fish's bulk through the sack. Boots off and back in the bag. You can't sleep at first because you are still reliving the capture. It's your personal best by far, and you can't wait to tell the world. What's that noise coming from the bushes behind the bivvy? It's probably only the bogey man so who gives a monkeys? 'Alright mate, cut it out! I've just caught a personal best.' Sweet dreams and sweet night fishing to you all!

▼ *As the sun breaks the skyline, a new day dawns. For Lee it's time to pack up and head off to work, leaving the fish in peace until his next session.*

Surface fishing

This is the most exciting and rewarding method known to the specimen carp angler

Your eyes glance across the lake's mirrored surface. A dark shape appears, followed by another, then another. Your eyes tune to the sight and you suddenly realise that the dark shapes are carp of various shapes and sizes. And some of them are big ones too.

You flick a tiny twig at them. It is quickly investigated and then rejected by one of the bigger fish. At this stage you realise that if they're willing to investigate a twig then they might just be more than willing to accept a bait fished on the surface. The problem is, you don't know how to go about doing it.

The obvious way is to fish for them with a small piece of free-lined bread crust but, although this is a successful method, when you return a little later with your tackle you find that the fish are now quite a bit further out into the lake and well out of range.

You give it your best shot though and hope that the fish will drift in a bit closer. The hoards of hungry rudd are making short work of your crust, all of which leads to regular recasting and constant disturbance of the swim, which has the effect of moving the

carp even further out of range. With a little thought and a bit of careful baiting, today could have been a red-letter day, instead of just another frustrating blank.

So where do you start when faced with a situation like this? First and foremost, surface fishing normally requires that you are mobile, so it's important to scale everything down so that you can move quickly, when necessary. What I normally do is to set up all my gear in a base camp somewhere on the lake and then seek out the fish with just my rod, landing net and my unhooking mat, carrying the minimum amount of tackle and bait required.

An essential item for surface fishing is a pair of good-quality polarised sunglasses. These help cut the glare off the lake's surface and make spotting fish much easier. Clothing can also make a difference. Easy-to-spot, bright colours like red and yellow are not ideal when trying to tempt a carp off the surface. Drab-coloured or even camouflaged clothing will help you to blend into the surroundings and make you less conspicuous to the carp. And with stealth you can sometimes get so close that you can almost touch them.

At all times avoid sudden movements

◄ *A pair of polarised sunglasses will help cut out the surface glare and also help spot fish drifting under the surface.*

like raising your arms as, although carp will not flinch if you remain still, sudden movements will nearly always alarm them.

For nearly all forms of surface fishing, apart from free-lining, some sort of float will be needed in order to give a bit of casting weight as well as giving you a visual indication of where your hook bait is. These floats are called controllers. They are made by a number of tackle manufacturers and are available in a variety of shapes and sizes.

Most controllers are a bit like self-cocking floats in that they have a weight attached to them to aid casting plus a very visually painted sight bob so that you can easily see them. Like all floats, there are certain light conditions in which darker colours are easier to see, so I normally carry a couple in my tackle box that have been painted black.

The size of controller float to use is obviously dictated by the distance you need to cast. Bigger controllers will obviously cast further, but they also make a much louder splash when they hit the surface, so I'd suggest using the smallest controller you can get away with to avoid spooking the fish. And another thing: try not to cast right on top of the fish, otherwise you're sure to scare them.

If the water's surface is calm, then try to cast beyond the fish and ever so gently inch the controller back into position. If it is a bit ruffled then try casting slightly to the side of

▲ *Drab clothing is vitally important when sneaking around, stalking carp off the surface.*

the fish so that the ripple drifts the float into position. The thing is, though, if there is a bit of a breeze blowing, the controller will continue to drift so this will mean recasting on a fairly regular basis in order to keep the float and bait in position.

Try to leave the float out for as long as possible because constant recasting is sure to alarm the fish. Bear in mind that unless the fish are holed up amongst a weed bed or are amongst lilies, then they're likely to move about the surface a bit, so

A SIMPLE BUBBLE FLOAT RIG

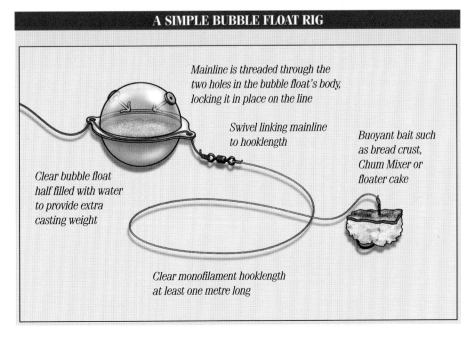

Mainline is threaded through the two holes in the bubble float's body, locking it in place on the line

Swivel linking mainline to hooklength

Buoyant bait such as bread crust, Chum Mixer or floater cake

Clear bubble float half filled with water to provide extra casting weight

Clear monofilament hooklength at least one metre long

▲ *A combination of intelligent feeding, stealth and concealment led to the downfall of this superb, 28lb-plus near-leather carp.*

even when your float drifts 'off the money' leave recasting until you're sure that your bait is a long way off the mark.

A mistake many anglers make when surface fishing (myself included) is to keep recasting in order to get back near to the fish. This normally leads to the fish becoming agitated and either moving to a different area or disappearing altogether. Be patient – you are more likely to succeed by waiting than by chasing the fish about with your float.

When surface fishing with a controller, try to keep your eye on the hook bait rather than the float. Many anglers expect to see the float soar across the surface in the event of a bite, but in my experience this is rarely the case. I normally try to keep my mainline fairly tight to the controller and am constantly taking up any slack line, and then the strike is made not when the float moves, but when the bait is

engulfed by the fish.

With regard to setting up a controller float, most of them have a swivel on the top for your mainline to pass through. Next, you need to tie on a small swivel to act as a stop, then comes your hooklink, which should be at least one metre long in order for your bait to behave naturally. Also, I always like to semi-fix my controller by having a sliding rubber float stop directly behind it on my mainline. This ensures that the hooklink swivel doesn't sink, which in turn causes the bait to drift towards the float and this sometimes also helps the hook 'prick' the carp as it comes up against the resistance, leading to a more positive take.

Hooklink material can be vitally important when fishing on the surface. Ordinary monofilament is a lot better than braid for this purpose, and the finer

the diameter, the more bites you'll generally get. Another material that I suspect could be good for surface fishing is fluorocarbon. I say suspect, because I haven't had the chance to try it for myself. But fluorocarbon has similar light refraction qualities to water, which means that it's less visible than normal line, so should be ideal for surface fishing.

Another set-up I've read about, but not yet tried, is a combination of ordinary mono with Kryston's open stranded Multi-Strand hooklink material. Multi-Strand is made of strands of a kevlar-type material that haven't been braided together and is perhaps the most supple hooklink material that has ever been produced. You need to use about two feet of ordinary mono for the swivel end of your hooklink and a foot of Multi-Strand at the hook end; the two are joined together by a simple loop to loop knot in much the same way as a hook to nylon is attached to your mainline.

Bait attachment needs a bit of thought when fishing on the surface with a controller, and a number of different anglers have their own preferred ways. Obviously if you're fishing with a bait such as bread crust, then

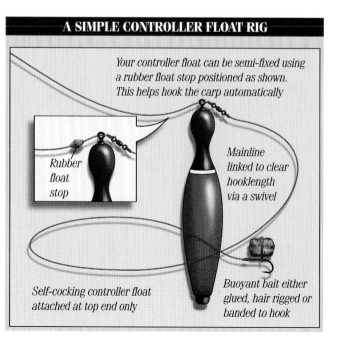

A SIMPLE CONTROLLER FLOAT RIG

Your controller float can be semi-fixed using a rubber float stop positioned as shown. This helps hook the carp automatically

Rubber float stop

Mainline linked to clear hooklength via a swivel

Self-cocking controller float attached at top end only

Buoyant bait either glued, hair rigged or banded to hook

this has to be presented with the hook inside. With baits such as Chum Mixers, however, you have a number of different options, all of which work to a degree. Some anglers mount their hook bait into a rubber bait band that is attached to the shank of the hook. Some glue the mixer to the back of the shank. And some present their bait on a very short hair rig. The latter is my favourite method, and what I generally do is to present two mixers on the hair after first drilling a hole through them with a nut drill.

Another alternative that I've tried with some success is to cut a slit into a 12mm cork ball, superglue the hook shank into it and then use this as a hook bait instead of a proper bait. Often, when using mixers, the carp take them with such gusto that they cannot possibly tell the difference between the cork ball and proper food. And because the cork ball is actually more buoyant it is sometimes one of the first 'baits' to be taken by the carp.

Correct feeding of your swim can be crucial when fishing with baits such as Chum Mixers. The main thing is not to be in too much of a rush to cast in. I always reckon that you are better off either just fishing with a single hook bait when fishing on the surface or building up the swim until the fish are really 'having it' before you cast out your hook bait. Again, patience is key. At first the carp might not show much interest in your free offerings, so to fish for them at this stage is even further lessening your chances.

Keep the free offerings trickling in. One or two might be taken at first or maybe none, because carp do not respond to surface food on all waters. If you get one or two fish feeding, more should join in. Keep feeding them and feeding them, building up their confidence. At this stage you should already have baited your hook in readiness for a cast,

because if you haven't you might now have a bit of trouble because your hands will be a quivering mess! They're really having it now and are racing each other to get to the next mixer. Now is the time to cast, but be

prepared, because you'll often get a bite straight away! You need to be a bit vigilant when playing the fish at this stage and steer it away from the rest of the shoal as quickly and as quietly as possible in order not to

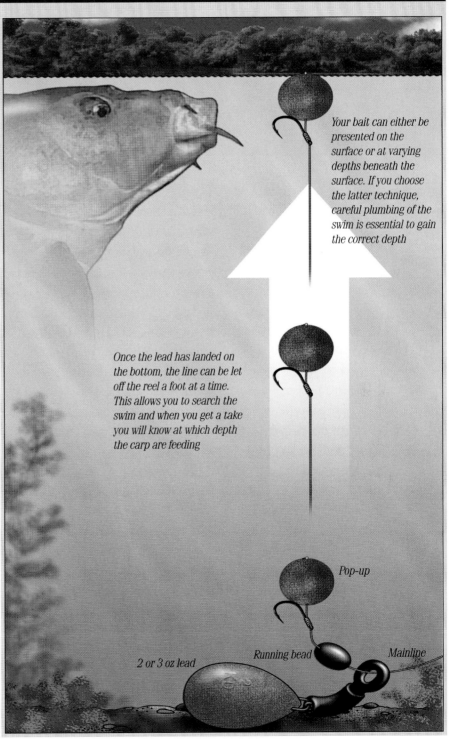

HOW TO PRESENT A RUNNING POP-UP

Your bait can either be presented on the surface or at varying depths beneath the surface. If you choose the latter technique, careful plumbing of the swim is essential to gain the correct depth

Once the lead has landed on the bottom, the line can be let off the reel a foot at a time. This allows you to search the swim and when you get a take you will know at which depth the carp are feeding

Pop-up

2 or 3 oz lead *Running bead* *Mainline*

◄ *Feeding is key when surface fishing. Trigger the fish's competitive instincts, have them fighting each other for the loose feed, and they are as good as yours!*

spook them. Chances are you could catch another if you've managed not to disturb them too much.

As soon as the fish is in the net, pick up the catapult and fire out some more free offerings. You're bound to be pleased with the carp you've just landed, but you'll be doubly pleased if you can smanage to land one or two more!

Another method of surface fishing, or rather fishing near the surface, that I've had a fair

▲ *One of the easiest ways of hooking dry Chum Mixers is to Superglue them to your hook. Saw a groove into the bait, drip glue into the groove and push in the hook shank. This process can be repeated with a cork ball too – a great alternative surface 'bait'.*

degree of success with in the past is to present a pop-up boilie on a long hooklink so that it's fished just below the water's surface. This really is a method that's best used on shallow waters less than four feet deep.

First of all, using a marker/depth finding set-up, find the depth of the area that you intend fishing. Then it's a simple case of using a hooklink that's marginally shorter than the depth. The hooklink is set up on a semi-fixed bolt rig set-up, just as you would when legering a boilie, except that the hooklink is far longer.

The good thing about this method is that it's not necessary to keep recasting, and you can fish with more than one rod at any one time. Another thing is that you can still fire out free offerings such as Chum Mixers in the vicinity of where you have cast, indeed it's normally beneficial to do so.

Again, as when using a controller, mono or fluorocarbon hooklinks seem favourite when using this method, with the pop-up fished on a very short hair rig.

Another alternative is to implement a free-running rig. This set-up consists of a

simple leger bomb, a swivel linked to the end of the mainline and a monofilment hooklength tied to it. The buoyant bait is then attached to the hook and allowed to float to the surface after casting. Although this is not technically a bolt rig set-up, when the carp takes the bait it will feel the hook point and bolt, hooking itself in the process.

Bite indication, when employing these methods, is exactly the same as when legering on the bottom, in that you set your rod on banksticks and use some form of visual indicator as well as maybe your bite alarms. As with controller fishing, keep the free offerings trickling in and try to steer any hooked fish away from the feeding area as quickly as possible so that you give yourself a chance of hooking another.

Float fishing for carp is very much a neglected method nowadays, although I suppose it's understandable with the modern-day desire to sit behind a nice neat-looking set-up incorporating two or three

▼ *A nut drill and baiting needle are absolutely essential if you intend hair rigging fresh, hard Chum Mixers.*

rods. There's nothing like a bit of float bashing for carp, however, and the sight of bubbles rising beside your float or the occasional little dip of your float can really set your heart pumping.

Another thing about float fishing for carp is that shotting patterns don't seem to be so crucial, and often a fairly crude set-up will produce the goods. This is just as well really, because it's a long time since I've done any match-fishing, so where my shot is positioned is more down to guesswork than being a well thought-out science!

When fishing in shallow water I would normally use a straight waggler float. After plumbing the depth with a plummet attached I normally put the bulk of my shot directly below the float and have a couple of smaller shot about six inches from the bait. It's hardly national championship stuff I know, but it gets me by and has helped me catch a few fish, including 30lb carp!

I suppose that the main time that I use a float is when I am stalking. Often a carp can become alarmed when a heavy lead is cast near to it. With a float, however, there is far less disturbance, and provided that you're quiet and remain reasonably well hidden, the carp should hardly know that you're there.

What I sometimes do is to bait up a few likely-looking close-in spots with a little hemp, or some sweetcorn, then creep round with my float to investigate. Often a carp or two will be in residence by the time you've returned to the first spot that you baited.

For fishing in deeper waters (those in excess of about six feet or so), I prefer to use one of these clever little floats that find their own depth, such as the Dave Thomas Locslides or the Polaris floats. All you do with these is to simply thread the float onto your line in the way suggested on the instructions, cast out, sink your mainline and then feed off

slack line until the float bobs to the surface. Once it has reached the surface it's a simple case of taking up slack in order to cock the float, as desired.

Admittedly, using this type of float is a bit like float legering and is perhaps not as sensitive as conventional float fishing. However, it really does come in handy if you want to move from swim to swim and don't wish to keep plumbing the depth each time.

So there you have it – a few tips which may help you to tempt a carp or two off the surface and on the bottom. So now it's time to put on the polarised sunglasses, grab a little bit of tackle and, with a pocket full of sandwiches and a cool bottle of pop, go and catch yourself a carp.

◀ Self locking floats, such as the Dave Thomas Locslide or Polaris (pictured left) are perfect for carp fishing in water deeper than 6ft as there is no need to plumb the depth and possibly spook the fish while doing so.

▼ All controller floats are self cocking and should be attached to the mainline top end only.

The tackle bag

A tour of Lee's tackle bag

▼ *For Method feeder fishing I always have a few bags of groundbait in the van just in case I need it. Also remember that Vitalin dog food is just as good and can be moulded around a feeder or bomb.*

▲ *ESP Bait stops are carried in two sizes.*

▲ *A stringer needle and a baiting needle are essential.*

▶ *Instead of a rucksack I've taken to using a large carryall bag as this fits nicely on the top of the Carp Porter trolley system I now use. It's not that I'm lazy and can't be bothered to carry my kit, it's a matter of fishing longer sessions and having to walk a fair old way to the swim (and I'm getting old). The bag is also big enough to carry everything I need, from tackle to toaster!*

▲ Here's a selection of the ingredients I use to make up fresh bait. My main mix is Solar Tackle's Club Mix. I make up a fresh batch of bait and keep them hanging in an air dry bag in the back of my van. If I make too much some of it can be frozen for use later on.

▲ You've got to eat well on the bank, and I use a stove to cook up an evening meal and a breakfast when I'm fishing nights. I even take along a wok and have become quite good at the old Indian cooking. The kettle allows me to boil up water for a cuppa. Cheers!

▲ Items I need for feature finding and feeding – like marker floats, spods, catapults and a throwing stick – are all kept together. Feature finding can save you a lot of time. I would suggest that on any new water you spend at least three days looking and plumbing before you fish.

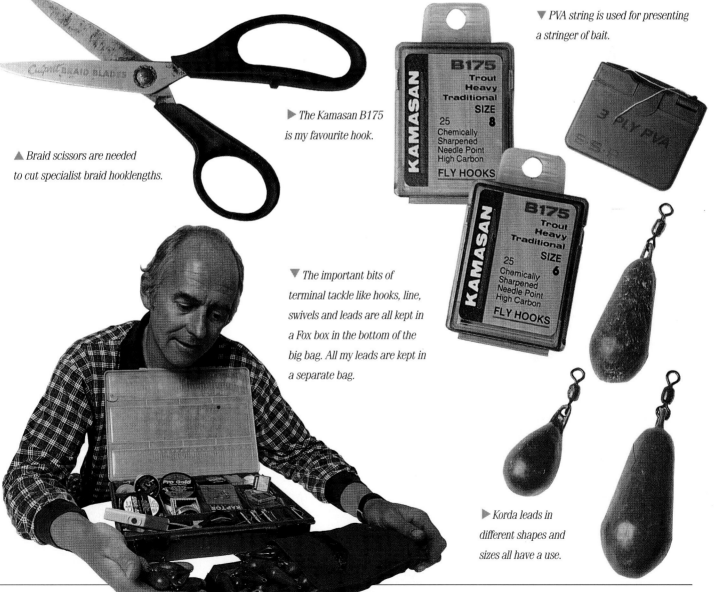

▼ PVA string is used for presenting a stringer of bait.

▲ Braid scissors are needed to cut specialist braid hooklengths.

▶ The Kamasan B175 is my favourite hook.

▼ The important bits of terminal tackle like hooks, line, swivels and leads are all kept in a Fox box in the bottom of the big bag. All my leads are kept in a separate bag.

▶ Korda leads in different shapes and sizes all have a use.

▲ For footwear I wear a pair of tough shoes to and from the session and sometimes during if the ground is dry. But I also carry a pair of short ankle boots and a pair of waders. The waders come in handy for margin work if the water is up and I have to wade out to net a fish.

▲ I also use a variety of shelf-life and frozen boilies, especially on new waters that I've not fished before. Also the frozen Tutti Frutti boilies are great baits for the winter as they leak off the flavour quickly. Other baits I carry are corn and shelf-life pop-ups.

▲ Pellets and hemp are great particle feeds for a spot of after-dark margin fishing. I carry a few mixed packs of pellets in the back of the van along with some pre-cooked hemp.

▶ Kevin Nash safety clip houses the swivel on the rig.

▲ Fox rig glue can be used to secure knots.

◀ Rig tube is used to protect the line above the hooklength.

▲ Richworth paste bombs for paste or Method fishing.

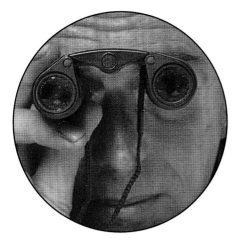

▲ During the day I like to scan the water for signs of moving fish. A good pair of compact binoculars are essential for this. I also carry a pair of polarised sunglasses for fish spotting at close range. You'll be surprised at what you can see when using polarised glasses.

▲ A head torch, candle lamp and small lighting box give me all the light I need for re-baiting and landing fish. The small box with two green lights is made by Black Box Solutions – the lights come on when I tap the top of the box. Keep your lights dull to avoid scaring fish.

▲ Here's my waterproof clothing. I use a camo coat from Realtree which has a detatchable inner fleece. It's waterproof and warm and this is essential on a cold night. I also carry a pair of ESP waterproof trousers as well as spare clothes just in case I get wet.

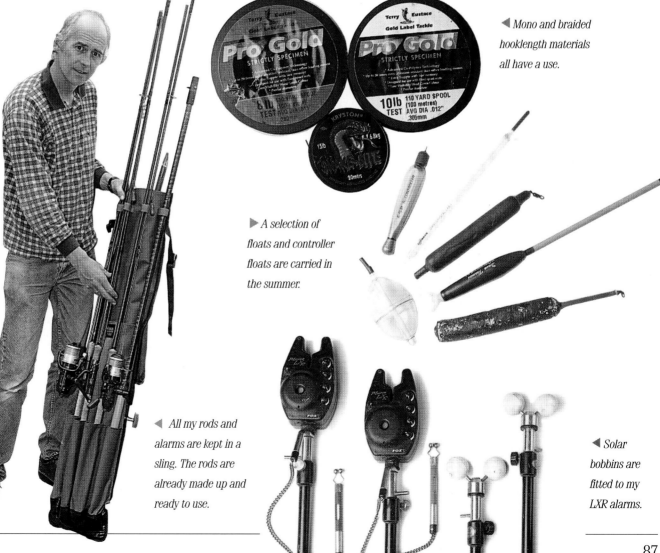

◀ Mono and braided hooklength materials all have a use.

▶ A selection of floats and controller floats are carried in the summer.

◀ All my rods and alarms are kept in a sling. The rods are already made up and ready to use.

◀ Solar bobbins are fitted to my LXR alarms.

Carp baits

Big particles, groundbait mixes, pellets, PVA and surface baits

Big particles

A number of different baits fall into my 'big particles' category, including the many different types of beans, peas and nuts as well as some more unusual types such as cockles and peeled prawns.

Of all of the beans, the most successful fish catchers over the years have been red kidney and blackeye beans, although there are obviously a lot of others that come close, such as borlotti beans and haricot beans, My favourites peas are chickpeas or maple peas. Both have accounted for some massive carp catches over the years.

In the past I've used a variety of particle baits and most have caught me some carp, although it has to be said that some have definitely been more effective than others. Perhaps my favourite particle baits of all time, and certainly the most effective, fall into the nut category, and in particular tiger nuts and peanuts.

Perhaps that's why they were named nuts in the first place, because carp definitely go nuts for them! With peanuts, though, you must ensure you use the 'human grade' variety, which can be bought in healthfood shops and suchlike. The type sold for bird feed are unsafe for fish.

The correct preparation of particle-type baits is of paramount importance, not only for them to be effective but also with the fish's welfare in mind. All beans, peas and nuts must be soaked in water for at least 12 hours prior to cooking to ensure that they take on water and swell up before being eaten by the fish. Obviously, if they are eaten prior to soaking they could swell up inside the fish, causing discomfort and in some cases death.

After soaking beans and peas, they need to be brought to the boil and then simmered for about 20 minutes to soften them, which makes them easier to use and more palatable for the fish. Tiger nuts need cooking for longer, although even then they remain relatively hard. Many carp anglers, myself

▲ Chickpeas and broken or chopped nuts make superb hook baits. All nut baits should be soaked for at least 24 hours, boiled and simmered for 30 minutes.

included, have often mused as to why hard baits such as tigers are so effective.

Personally I believe this is for two reasons. Firstly, I think they taste really nice and are very 'more-ish'. Secondly, I think that carp like the 'crunch'. It could also be that passing hard foods through their digestive system acts like eating roughage, and helps clear their systems out. Certainly in captivity I've seen carp pass small stones out of their vents. Have they eaten them by mistake or have they eaten them for a purpose? Whatever the case, in my opinion tiger nuts are the most effective carp catching particle bait of all time, whatever the reason that carp eat them.

◄ Whole 'jumbo' tiger nuts are a top bait in winter and summer. For added attraction, add 15ml of liquid Talin (sweetener) to the nuts as they soak. To hook single tiger nuts they must be threaded onto the hair lengthways.

Another reason tigers are good is that carp are selective, and apart from the occasional pioneering bream or tench, it's only really carp that seem to like them, a big advantage if your water contains a lot of so called 'unwanted' species such as eels. Peanuts are another stunning particle. I find peanuts to be most effective when they have been just soaked, without being boiled at all, again it might be because they are crunchier when eaten like this.

Other nuts such as brazils, almonds and hazelnuts have also accounted for their fair share of carp over the years and are prepared in much the same way as tigers. These can be well worth a try by way of a change.

Seafood baits? Yummy! Cockles, prawns and shrimps are all baits that carp love, although I don't get to use them very often because I cannot keep from eating them myself. So there you have it. A few particle baits to try out. There may be times when baits like boilies are most convenient, but believe you me, on occasions particles are the bait that you really can 'Bag up' on.

PVA

PVA is an abbreviation of Poly Vinyl Acetate, a substance that dissolves if it gets wet or comes into contact with moisture. In fishing, and especially in carp fishing, it has a multitude of uses. These predominantly revolve around presenting free offerings in close vicinity to your hook bait in order to draw attention to it.

Whether you choose string, tape, bags or tubes, it is available in two different forms, one of which resembles polythene and the other of which is like stocking-net cloth.

That said, however, Kryston Products have just brought out a range of PVA products called the Meltex range. These have a ribbed polythene appearance that is very strong and I can see them becoming very popular.

It goes without saying that when using PVA for whatever reason it should be used in a totally dry environment. Things like your hands, bait and end tackle need to be dry, otherwise the PVA has a good chance of partially dissolving before you have had a chance to cast it into the lake.

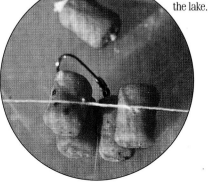

The main use for PVA is for tying up what is known as a 'stringer'. This involves threading some free offerings onto a length of PVA string or tape by way of a long baiting needle known as a stringer needle. This is then secured over the bend of your hook just prior to casting out.

Another clever way of tying up a stringer was shown to me by carp supremo Terry Hearn, and this involves using small cylindrical-shaped baits, threading three or four of these onto a length of PVA string and then tying the presentation tightly around your hooklink, above your hook. Once tied, and once the loose ends of the string are neatly trimmed off, this is slipped down your hooklink until it comes to rest on the shank of your hook.

The main advantage of this method is that when fishing in amongst weed, because the free baits partially hide the hook point, they prevent the point from getting masked by the weed. Stringers are perfect for presenting bigger free offerings such as boilies. For smaller food items such as pellets, dryish particles like tiger nuts and peanuts, or natural baits such as casters, bags or tubes offer a distinct advantage.

It is possible to present PVA tubes or bags full of freebies in a number of different ways. With the stocking type you can fill them up with free offerings, tie the top with some PVA string and then clip your hook under the knot just prior to casting. With the polythene type you can present your lead weight inside the bag along with the freebies. This comes in useful if fishing in weed.

The dissolving time of PVA really depends on two things, the gauge of the PVA and the temperature of the water. Whatever way though, it should take no more than about a few minutes to dissolve and release the free offerings. If fishing

a deep water with depths in excess of around 15 feet, I always prefer to use the thicker gauge PVA bags because I'm sure that sometimes with the thinner type the free offerings drop out before it has reached the lake bed.

For me the best type of bags to use in deep water are those produced by Kevin Nash Tackle. They are a lot thicker than normal and so give you a bit of leeway even to pull it back into position if you so wish. Finally, there are a few obscure uses for PVA. I sometimes PVA a poly-ball or a wine bottle cork to my hook just prior to casting. Once dissolved, the polyball or cork rises to the surface, giving me a good visual marker to fire out free offerings towards.

Wrapping a piece of the polythene-type PVA tape around your hook helps to stop your hook from getting masked by weed. Or PVA your hook bait to a clip up above your anti-tangle tubing. This helps streamline your end tackle, gaining a few extra yards when fishing at very long range. PVA – it's a useful bit of equipment to have in your tackle box.

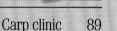

Groundbait mixes

As with all types of carp bait additives and attractors, the number of different Method feeder groundbaits now available has reached huge proportions.

Perhaps my favourite groundbait combination that I have used with a lot of success is a 50/50 mixture of Van Den Eynde's Method Mix and their Hi-Pro Carp groundbaits. The resulting mixture has a nice sweet, fruity smell that all bottom-feeding species seem to like.

Nowadays we are faced with a lot more choice: as well as the renowned groundbait-producing companies such as Sensas and Whizzo, many of the carp-bait companies are coming out with Method feed groundbaits of their own. Examples are Rod Hutchinson's Monster Mix, no doubt based on their very effective Monster Crab flavouring, or the new Specialist Carpet Feed groundbait from Nutrabaits,

which is hemp-based. Others are the new Method mixes from Nashbaits, and the specialist Method mixes from Richworth. These are all very effective, so it's really a case of what takes your fancy.

One effective groundbait that is still on the official secret-list in many carping circles is not even produced by a fishing bait manufacturer, but is sold for you to feed your dog. It's called Vitalin dog food. The good thing about Vitalin is that not only is it very effective, but it is also economical in comparison to others – a great big sack of the stuff can be bought from a pet superstore for under £15. The crazy thing with Vitalin is that at a glance you would never believe you could make groundbait out of it. It contains great big lumps of flaked maize that look like cornflakes, as well as oats and all manner of other different bits and pieces. Yet you simply mix water with it and it binds together to mould around a frame feeder, and withstands full-blast casting! Carp absolutely love

the stuff. You can mix all manner of different things with it in order to try and make it even more effective, although this is applies with any groundbait. Things like fishmeal, trout pellet powder, garlic granules, sugar and chili powder can all be tried to give that extra 'oomph'. Don't be afraid to experiment because you might just come up with something a bit special! One of my favourite additions is a bird food called Robin Red, which is sold by John E. Haith seed merchants of Cleethorpes. Robin Red is one of the best carp bait attractors, no matter in what form of carp bait it is included, and in Vitalin it is stunning! You only need to include a small amount and the resulting ground bait mixture will turn from a dull-looking oatmeal colour to an attractive, bright red. Even at the tender age of eight , it seemed to me that the most effective groundbaits were coloured red. Anyone out there remember Kestral? No surely not, you can't be that old!

As well as powdered additives, various liquids and oils can be included in groundbaits as well as water to bind the mix together: things like Corn Steep Liquor, sesame seed oil, Camp coffee (ask your grandad if you don't know what it is), liquidised sweetcorn – the choices are endless. The thing is about adding oil, such as sesame, is that because it does not mix with water, droplets of oil rise to the surface, along with particles of groundbait, thus further expanding the area of attraction. This oil slick can also be used to your advantage. Firstly it can be used as a marker for any free boilies you want to introduce straight after casting, and secondly if carp move onto the feed they often disturb the mix and send an oil slick to the surface, giving their presence away in the process.

And what about adding some live food such as maggots or casters or perhaps some pellets – they all work! I'll tell you what, all of this talk of different groundbait additives has prompted me to lock the kitchen door (in case 'er indoors catches me out) raid the cupboards, and see what I can find. Baked beans, pizza, Ovaltine, dhansak sauce, jalfrezi sauce, mmmn? Where's the Vitalin? I think I might just creep out of the back door and go fishing now!

STEP-BY-STEP: LOADING UP A RICHWORTH PASTE BOMB

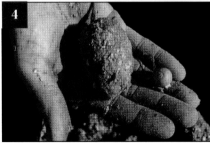

1 Lee's mix for the paste bomb set-up is a dog food called Vitalin.
2 The paste bomb is fitted to a safety clip and is fished in the 'on-the-side' manner, as shown.

3 The Vitalin dog food is mixed with water and moulded around the paste bomb.
4 With the paste bomb completely covered it's time to cast out the rig.

Pellets

J udging by the vast number of different pellets available, you'd have thought that they were a relatively new thing in carp fishing. However, nothing could be further from the truth.

I can remember things like trout pellets and other pellets such as rabbit pellets being used to good effect for carp back in the early 1970s!

I've got to be honest and state that sometimes it seems to me that the entire carp world has gone pellet mad, and I for one don't really know what all the fuss is about.

When you consider what pellets do once they settle on the lake bed (they break down to resemble groundbait), then why not use groundbait instead, because a ball of this can certainly be fired out a lot further than pellets? That said, however, pellets are here to stay and can be a useful addition to a carp fisher's armoury.

They are excellent for fishing alongside your hook bait in PVA bags and they are excellent for mixing in with seed baits, such as hemp, in order to increase the attraction. They are also good for holding fish in a swim without filling them up.

As I said, there are vast numbers of different types of pellets now available, all of which work to some degree or other.

It's now possible to buy pellets to match some of the boilies that are on sale, which obviously increases the attraction around your hook bait.

Up until recently most of the pellets available were based around trout feed pellets, but it has since come to light that the high oil content of these type of pellets might not be good for a carp's health if eaten in excess.

My favourite pellets are the Formula Magic pellets produced by Rod Hutchinson and Relum. These pellets are made up of ground down versions of things that carp really like, such as tiger nuts, peanuts, maize and hemp, to name but a few.

Also they are small, therefore they can be catapulted right on top of the fish without really disturbing them. In fact it often has the reverse effect and sets them off feeding.

Other pellets – such as the Mainline Response pellets, our own Tackle Box Mighty Ming pellets, or the Essential Products Shellfish B5 pellets – rely on breaking down and releasing large amounts of water-soluble attractors into the swim. Therefore, the dissolving scents pull fish in from a greater area.

The Nutrabaits Total Hemp pellets are made up of almost pure hemp seed, and we all know how effective this is. The big advantage with these is that they can be fired out a lot further than it is possible to fire hemp seed.

Then you have ball pellets. These are normally around 18mm in diameter and, being perfectly spherical, can be fired out to extreme distances if that is what is required. Like a lot of the other pellets, ball pellets are extremely good because they break down fairly quickly and leave a lot of 'scent' in the area of your hook bait. They do not offer very much in the way of food though, and the carp often grub around in the area until they find some, and hopefully this will be your hook bait.

▲ Smaller, soft pellets can be used directly on the hook and are a great bait for small carp.

It's a bit like walking down the street and smelling eggs and bacon cooking. You might not have been hungry before, but you sure as hell are now and you cannot wait to get into the cafe! This is what you are trying to do in most forms of fishing, apart from lure and fly fishing where you are trying to antagonise a fish into taking your bait.You are laying down a scent trail that is hopefully screaming out FOOD! This is why pellets are often so good because they can shout out louder than most feeds!

▲ Bigger pellets should be fished on a hair-rig like this.

Surface baits

Possibly the best-known surface bait of modern times are dog biscuits – Pedigree Chum Mixers. I often wonder if the makers of these realise how many packets of their products have been scattered over the surface of lakes and other waters all around the country. Maybe dogs have had to go hungry now and again but the carp certainly haven't!

Something has happened with Chum Mixers in recent years, because they are now nowhere near as buoyant as they used to be and often just the weight of the hook is enough to sink them. Never fear though, because help is near as that nice Mr Tesco has brought out a version of his own which is far more buoyant.

Most of the time I prefer to use Mixers straight from the packet and exactly as they come, but many anglers like to add a flavour combination of their own. To do this simply place some Mixers onto a riddle or in a sieve. Pour some hot water over the biscuits, making sure all the baits have received a soaking. Now place the biscuits into a thick polythene bag and add your chosen flavour and colour, give the bag a shake and leave to cool.

As the biscuits cool, they will draw in the flavour and the colour. Prepared like this, the Mixers should swell a little and soften, so they should not need drilling to present them on your hook.

As well as Mixers there are a number of other cat or dog biscuits that can be tried on the surface, in fact most of these float, so the permutations are almost endless. One minute you could try the fish-shaped Go Cat biscuits, the next you could try the giant-sized biscuits designed for feeding Mr Doberman!

As well as the dog and cat biscuits there are loads of other foods that float and that could be useful for catching carp off the surface. Breakfast cereals such as Sugar Puffs, sunflower seeds, pop corn and various pond fish pellets are all good, in fact I could go on and on. And not forgetting bread, which was covered in Carp baits 1 (see page 25). Bread crust is a fantastic surface bait and one which has produced countless carp over the years and will no doubt continue to do so in the future.

And then you have home-made floater cake. This is far tougher than ordinary bread, but no less attractive. Floater cake can be made from practically any boilie base mix. Normally all that's required is to double up on the amount of eggs that you would normally use, in other words, if you would use six eggs to a pound of base mix, use 12 instead. Also add double the recommended dose of attractors, and then tip this sloppy mixture into a non-stick loaf tin and bake in the oven for roughly 90 minutes on gas Mark five (375°F/190°C). It's also worth adding a teaspoon or two of baking powder to the mix as this will help the cake to rise. You may need to experiment with cooking times in order to get it right and it might be worth asking for advice from mum!

Pop-up boilies are another bait which can be used as a surface floater although unless you are prepared to painstakingly roll them up very small, then they generally come second to all of the above.

So there you have it, visit the pet shop, the baker or the supermarket – all around you are foodstuffs that float and foodstuffs that a wily old carp will willingly gulp down off the surface.

STEP-BY-STEP: PREPARING CHUM MIXERS

1 You will need baits, a strong plastic bag, riddle, flavouring, colouring and a kettle.
2 Place a handful of Chum Mixers onto a riddle and pour boiling water over the top.
3 Tip the baits into the plastic bag and add a little of your chosen flavouring.
4 While the baits are still damp add your chosen powdered colouring.
5 Seal the bag and give the baits a really good shake. Leave to cool for an hour.
6 The finished product will stand out from the rest of the loosefeed like a sore thumb!

Questions and answers

Lee answers some of your questions

What sort of things will I need to take into account when fishing over gravel?

When fishing over gravel you really need to be looking at protecting the end tackle from the sharp bottom elements as much as possible. Rig tubing is without doubt a must to protect the line above the rig from being cut on the sharp gravel bars. Gravel bars in particular are renowned for shearing an unprotected mainline as a carp bolts off over the bar. The hook is also under threat from being blunted by chippings of gravel as it lands on the bottom. I use a nugget of Solar dissolving foam, which is impaled over the

▼ Rig tube will protect your mainline against sharp gravel bars.

▲ A nugget of Solar dissolving foam protects the point of the hook. Once dissolved it will leave the hook clear and clean.

hook point before casting. Once the rig has reached the bottom, the foam does two jobs. Firstly it slows the descent of the hook, and secondly it remains in place for a short time after entering the water before dissolving. Once dissolved the hook is left unmarked and free from any form of hindrance. I also favour a shorter hooklength to get a more positive connection when the carp picks up the bait. On casting

I always feel the lead down to the bottom to ensure I've landed the bait on a clean, hard surface. Obviously if you have plumbed up and used a marker float to identify the area you'll know it is clear.

When fishing over weed how do you get the hook bait into a suitable position?

Fishing over weed is not something many newcomers to carp fishing try. It's a shame really, because there are often more carp in amongst the sanctuary of weed than there are in the open water. A bit of confidence

▼ A big lead will help to bomb the bait down through the weed. Pop-ups or balanced baits can be used to sit the bait up above or on top of the weed. A longer hooklength made from mono line can help with some weed presentations.

mixed with good rig presentation will see far more runs and more fish on the bank. If it's silk weed you are looking to tackle, I suggest you use a longer hooklength and a balanced bait. This set-up, combined with a balanced bait, will allow the bait to rest on top of the weed and not in it. When I say a balanced bait, I mean a bait that has a foam insert placed through the core to make it partly buoyant. I also incorporate a light lead with this rig. The light lead helps with presentation and stops the bait being pulled tight into the weed. With heavy weed beds you are often better off trying to bomb a bait through them to a clear area. To do this you will need to use a heavier lead. A shorter hooklength is also used to ensure the hook bait follows the line of the lead as it goes through the weed. Once the cast has been made I feel the lead down and wait to feel the bump of the lead landing on a clear patch of bottom. Once again I rely on Solar dissolving foam to mask the hook point. PVA is another option that's worth looking at. It's not something I use a lot but it can get your lead and rig down through the weed in one hit. I would suggest you look at the solid bag types that are available. Make sure you expel all the air from the bag before sealing it and casting. Trapped air will cause the bag to float and it will end up dissolving before it has reached the target area.

What sort of presentation would you use over silt?

When faced with presenting a bait over silt I favour a flat lead. In fact I go as far as flattening my own to attain a greater surface area on the lead. The bigger the surface area of the lead, the less likely it is to sink deep into the silt. Therefore the

bait won't get dragged down below the silt and hidden from view. I also opt for the longer hooklength again as this keeps the bait up out of the silt. With the longer hooklength in use I employ a balanced bait in the knowledge that the bait is sitting on top of the silt. I balance the bait by inserting a cork or foam core after hollowing out the centre of the boilie. If there are any fragments of weed on the bottom it's worth masking the hook again with dissolving foam. Mono or braided hooklengths fished with a balanced bait score well. If you are using a bottom bait you need to try and gauge how deep the silt is, as you don't want the bait sinking right down into it. Pop-up baits are another alternative which combat the bottom elements and also create a visual bait.

When would you use a pop-up instead of a bottom bait?

Pop-ups are a great opportunity bait, and used as a single bait with no feed and placed on known patrol routes they are often taken out of sheer curiosity. I also recommend them as a single bait in winter. I get to fish a variety of waters throughout the year and like you may not have fished them before. My first plan of action on a water in winter would be to fish with a single hook bait popped up off the bottom. For bottom baits in winter I favour a Tutti Frutti (Richworth frozen) 14mm. Fruit flavours are best in the winter as they are able to leak off the flavour a lot

quicker. In the warmer months I make up a mix of Solar's Perfect Pop-up and add fish flavours, and for bottom baits I like the Solar Club Mix. The height the pop-up is positioned off the bottom is down to personal choice. In the summer you might have to position the bait slightly higher, up to 18 inches, to combat bottom weed, yet in the winter the weed should have died back and a bait positioned one to two inches off the bottom might be more effective.

When fishing a new water for the first time what sort of baiting plan would you use?

With any new water I think the first thing you need to try and establish is how many fish are in there and where they are. I suggest you spend a few hours on the bank without your rods and ask questions of other anglers fishing the water. Be prepared to do something different as this could just pay off big time. If everyone is using a certain bait and you know what the mix is, try a different bait or the same mix with different flavours. I would elect to fish with three rods so I'm able to experiment with two or three different baits. One rod would have a single pop-up on it and would be cast to the centre of the lake and no free offerings would be presented around it. The other two rods would both be baited with bottom baits, and once cast I would then fire out around 20 to 30 free offerings of bait around each of the hook baits. No further freebies would be fed until a run or capture had occurred. If I was on the water for a night session I would also consider the marginal area. I often use a particle feed of Ming Pellets which I feed by hand into the margins. As darkness falls I position one rod slightly back from the edge of the bank, and

▲ *Flat leads and Solar dissolving foam are two favoured components when fishing over weed, gravel and silt.*

drop the hook bait into the margins. I have caught countless carp doing this because at night they often come right into the margins to feed. Margin stalking can also pay off if you can see the carp. It's worth noting down patrol routes and laying an ambush of bait and feed at some point along this trail. Whichever approach you take, remember to be sensible on the bait application. Don't just chuck it and chance it, plan it out and catch!

What determines the style and size of lead that you use?

The presentation you wish to use and the type of bottom area you are fishing over will both have to be taken into consideration when making a lead choice. Also you must ask yourself how much weight will be required to cast to the area you wish to fish. Having said that a heavy lead may also be required when fishing at short range to act as resistance on a bolt rig. There is also the way in

which the weight is fitted to the line. Some anglers prefer to fish the in-line method, where the line is threaded through the core of the lead and then a swivel sits up inside the lead, forming a semi-fixed set-up. Others, including myself, prefer the use of a safety clip to attach the lead in the 'on the side' position. The clips I use for this are the Kevin Nash type, which again hold the weight in a semi-fixed position. Most of my own fishing is usually done with a 2oz–2.5oz Korda distance weight (elongated pear). I find I can cast these further than the in-line style of lead. There are occasions though when a different style of lead will be needed to do a specific job. For example, if I were fishing up the side of a gravel bar I would incorporate a flat-sided lead to enable the lead to grip. I flatten off a Korda pear lead in a vice until it's really flat! The size of the lead will be dictated by the distance you want to cast. For increased distance I will, however, step these up to 3oz-4oz. I've also mentioned the use of a big lead at short range to act as a resistance bolt when fishing a bolt rig. This can be as much as 4oz and is usually fished in conjunction with a short hooklength. This ensures the carp comes in contact with the weight of the lead more or less as it picks up the bait. There are times when a light weight of say 1oz can be used on a free-running rig to give a resistance-free set-up. The take on this can be a steady rise of the bobbin as the carp swims off not realising it's been hooked.

What sort of hook pattern do you think is best?

This is one of the most popular questions that I get asked and there isn't really a correct answer. What I mean by this is that every hook maker in the country will claim that their hooks are the best, even if they aren't. What I will say is that I have used a pattern called the B175 made by Kamasan. It's a pattern developed for the fly angler and it has a long shank and is also extremely sharp. I use the hook because I have confidence in it and I haven't had any problems with presentations or fish losses. At the end of the day there are thousands of hooks out there and it's down to you to make a choice you are happy and confident with. Manufacturers like Drennan, ESP, Partridge, Fox, Kamasan and Nash all make good hooks which are firm favourites of many of the top carp anglers. The choice is yours!

Tailpiece

At some time or other most people grab a fishing rod in the hope of trying to catch a fish. To some, it becomes boring, and so it's given up in favour of knocking a little ball down a little hole in the grass, or kicking a bag of wind about a pitch for 90 minutes.

For the honoured few, however, fishing will become a way of escape, a way to make great friends and a way to become at one with nature.

I hope you've enjoyed and learned something from this book. It's time for me now to get some baits made and rigs tied, ready for my next session!

See you on the bank!

Lee Jackson